THE LITTLE LEAGUE® GUIDE TO
CONDITIONING AND TRAINING

PREPARING YOUNG PLAYERS
with Fundamentals and Basics

MARK GOLA

McGraw·Hill

New York Chicago San Francisco Lisbon London Madrid Mexico City
Milan New Delhi San Juan Seoul Singapore Sydney Toronto

Library of Congress Cataloging-in-Publication Data

Gola, Mark.
     The little league guide to conditioning and training / by Mark Gola.
        p.   cm.
     ISBN 0-07-142359-1
     1. Little League baseball.   2. Little League baseball—Training. I. Title.

   GV880.5.G65   2004
   796.357′62—dc22   2003018015

1 2 3 4 5 6 7 8 9 0 AGM/AGM 3 2 1 0 9 8 7 6 5 4

ISBN 0-07-142359-1

Interior photographs by Michael Plunkett

McGraw-Hill books are available at special quantity discounts to use as premiums and sales promotions, or for use in corporate training programs. For more information, please write to the Director of Special Sales, Professional Publishing, McGraw-Hill, Two Penn Plaza, New York, NY 10121-2298. Or contact your local bookstore.

This book is printed on acid-free paper.

This book is dedicated to Randy Voorhees,
the best of friends,
for making me a better person.

Contents

Contents

Acknowledgments

I would like to thank several individuals who were integral to putting this book on the shelf. Matthew Carnicelli, acquiring editor at McGraw-Hill, for his support and belief in this concept. Mandy Huber, assistant editor, for her guidance throughout the project, and for improving the presentation of this book.

Michael Plunkett, photographer, for his expertise in taking all the instructional photographs and for his friendship.

Randy Voorhees, for his information and advice on pitching instruction and general knowledge of the game.

Brendan Eccleston and the Manalapan Patriots, for their participation in the photo shoot: Brian Fenske, Patrick Younghans, Matthew Luongo, Chris Maglione, James Eccleston, Zachary Robbins, Kevin Petrone, Tyler Haines, Nick Yuhas, Mario Mennella, Glenn Edwards, and Jared Macher.

Chris Juffee, for her editorial review and suggestions in the first aid section of the book.

Dave Gallagher, for giving me the opportunity to earn a living working with youth league baseball players and coaches.

Edward F. Gola and Bill Cane, for volunteering their valuable time to coach young ballplayers when I played Little League baseball for Weidel Real Estate.

Introduction

This book is written to parents and coaches of Little League players who share their time to coach children. Its purpose is to assist coaches in teaching young ballplayers the game of baseball, how to improve their play, how to prepare for games physically and mentally, and how to keep the game safe and enjoyable. *The Little League Guide to Conditioning and Training* is a teacher's manual that presents parents with the information they need to become knowledgeable, organized, effective baseball coaches.

The book is divided into four easy-to-read sections that answer many of the questions Little League coaches often ponder. How much should a pitcher throw during warm-ups? When is the right time to bunt? How do you talk to a batter who is afraid of the ball? Should I teach a curveball to my best pitcher? What safety measures should I take at practice? Through countless hours of research, experience, and speaking with Little League coaches and parents, I have developed a presentation of information that discusses the most pertinent topics specific to Little League coaches and players.

Part 1, "Preseason Conditioning," focuses on preparing players for tryouts and the opening day of Little League. Teaching the basic fundamentals of hitting, pitching, and fielding are addressed in detail and enforced through the dozens of drills and exercises given at the end of each subject. A two-week training schedule for each part of the game (hitting, pitching, and fielding) is designed to prepare players so they start their season in top form.

Part 2, "Game-Day Routine," discusses pregame rituals and how to best prepare a team so they're ready at the first pitch. Stretching exercises, running form, drills, and pregame infield/outfield practice are among the many responsibilities coaches must undertake to get their team ready to play. Add to that getting the pitcher ready, writing and reading the starting lineup, going over ground rules with the umpire, and giving a pregame pep talk, and you'll understand why properly utilizing assistant coaches by delegating assignments is strongly recommended. This is another topic discussed in this section.

Evaluating strengths and weaknesses in players during the season and how to iron out the wrinkles during practice are topics addressed in Part 3, "In-Season Maintenance." Pitchers who struggle with control, batters who can't hit an outside strike, outfielders who have difficulty going back on fly balls—these problems surface on every Little League team. The goal during practices is to work on solving those problems. Also, certain plays like rundowns and defending first-and-third steals that occur during the game can be costly if not executed correctly. This section offers a blueprint design in how to prepare for these situational plays.

The final section, Part 4, "Keeping It Safe," is devoted to safety on the baseball field. Basic emergency procedures for injury and illness are perhaps the biggest responsibility that rests upon the shoulders of youth-league coaches and parents. Coaches should be equipped with contact information, first aid supplies, and the medical history of each player. In addition, there are certain plays during a baseball game in which injuries most frequently occur. Simple tips and suggestions are given to heighten safety on these plays and avoid potential injuries.

Many interesting sidebar topics, such as the adverse effects of hitting off pitching machines, how to break in a new baseball glove, and how to impress coaches at a tryout are sprinkled throughout the interior of this book. More than 125 photographs accompany the text to illustrate instructional advice and supply the reader with visual imagery.

The information throughout these pages will increase and enhance parents' knowledge with regard to coaching baseball. But more important than teaching a child how to hit a curveball or when to call for a squeeze play, or teaching a catcher how to block a ball, is that players have fun. Little League baseball provides an environment for young ballplayers to experience the fruits of the game in its purest form. Maintain focus that the primary reason for coaching is to assist children in their understanding and enjoyment of the game. If you accomplish that, then no matter what your record reads at the end of the season, you're a great Little League coach in our book.

Best of luck.

The Little League® Parent/Volunteer Pledge

I will teach children to play fair and do their best.

I will positively support all managers, coaches, and players.

I will respect the decisions of the umpires.

I will praise a good effort despite the outcome of the game.

The Manalapan Patriots baseball team

PART 1

PRESEASON CONDITIONING

GEARING UP FOR THE SEASON

Throughout every major-league baseball season, there are several absolutes that ballplayers, coaches, and fans can rely on. The National Anthem will be performed before each game. Some players will exceed expectations, while others will produce disappointing results. The season is interrupted by a midsummer classic (the All-Star Game) and culminates with the Fall Classic (the World Series). And every February, major-league baseball players and minor leaguers alike travel to Florida and Arizona to participate in spring training.

Players use spring training for various reasons. Some use it to eliminate rust and ready themselves for the season. Many players hope to embellish a specific aspect of their game, whether it's to hit for more power, improve defensive play, or develop a new pitch in their repertoire. Others are competing for a roster spot and hope to make an impression on management to secure a position on a major-league club.

Whatever the player's focus might be, spring training presents players with the opportunity to polish and prepare for competition. No professional player—not one—would dismiss spring training as useless and rather start the regular season immediately. Hall of Fame pitching legend Sandy Koufax once said, "People who write about spring training not being necessary never tried to throw a baseball." Preseason training and conditioning gives players the necessary time to prepare physically, mentally, and emotionally for the upcoming season.

Why the overkill on selling the importance of major-league spring training? Consider this. If major-league baseball players—the very best baseball players in the world—recognize the importance of preseason training, imagine how valuable it is to Little League baseball players. Preseason conditioning provides youth players with the time to get into "baseball shape," establish a solid foundation of fundamentals, and develop comfort and confidence out on the baseball field.

The equation is simple. Preparation breeds confidence, and confidence breeds success. Whether it's in science class or playing Sony PlayStation, kids respond positively when they see themselves getting better at something and succeeding. Individual and team success on the baseball field will only enhance kids' enjoyment playing the game.

To pitch effectively, pitchers must condition their arms before the start of the season.

Preparing the Baseball Muscles

An athlete who is in exceptional physical condition is not necessarily prepared to play baseball. Strength enhances player performance, yet youth-league bats generally weigh little over a pound and balls weigh only five ounces. Running speed and endurance have merit, yet the farthest Little

League base runners travel is 240 feet—and that's if they hit an inside-the-park home run! Baseball is a sport that requires explosive movements. It's about creating arm speed, bat speed, and having quickness and agility.

Getting the body into baseball shape requires repetitious training in executing the proper fundamental movements. What is the best way for hitters to generate better bat speed and hit with more power? By taking swing after swing after swing—the right way. How do pitchers develop greater arm strength? By throwing with more regularity—the right way. Can shortstops increase their throwing range from season to season? Absolutely. By taking countless ground balls to the right and left, but doing so the correct way to develop a more explosive first step to the ball.

Baseball has been played for over 100 years, and there are very few secrets looming that lead to instant performance enhancement. Parents and coaches often search for a quick fix or some type of overpriced gadget that will bear immediate results. But the bottom line is this: players must work on perfecting their technique first. Once they have accomplished that, they can then move forward practicing that technique repeatedly—hundreds and thousands of times. That is the primary way to improve baseball skills. If a player's throwing technique (for example) is flawed, through hours of practice that player will only become good at throwing the wrong way.

Getting into baseball shape and developing fundamentally sound mechanics also reduces the risk of injury. Good fielding, throwing, and hitting mechanics allow players to maximize power and consistency, and also minimize any unnecessary strain on the body. A pitcher might have a great arm in spite of poor throwing mechanics, but in time, some part of his or her body will break down due to unnecessary stress. The memorable experiences of having success on the mound will eventually be overshadowed by injury and an inability to compete. Good mechanics improve the way kids play the game, but more important, they keep them healthy and on the field.

A Psychological Edge

There is no question that preseason conditioning prepares the body for competition. Equally important, however, is that players strengthen their psyche during training. Let's use hitting as an example. Taking dry swings daily (swinging the bat with no pitch thrown) improves bat speed. Hitters will be able to get the barrel of the bat from their stance position to the hitting zone more quickly and with greater authority. Hitting off of a batting tee enables hitters to address flaws in their swing and then iron out the wrinkles. Doing soft-toss drills improves hand-to-eye coordination and gives hitters a better feel for how to get the barrel of the bat to the middle of the ball with greater consistency. Taking batting practice allows hitters to establish timing and to understand their personal strengths on pitch locations.

All of these elements combine to form a foundation of confidence. No physical skill bears more importance to a hitter than confidence. Size, strength, quickness, and hand-to-eye coordination all take a backseat to confidence. Confidence allows the body to perform at its very best. Without it, a player's actions are timid, apprehensive, and/or indecisive. Pitchers, infielders, hitters, and base runners must be confident to maximize their capabilities and optimize results.

Repetitious training heightens a player's comfort level, which enhances confidence. Practicing over and over again also develops "muscle memory." Muscle memory means the body reacts to a situation without hesitation. It just does it. Baseball is a very fast game—a game of reactions. The thinking process occurs before the ball is put into play. Pitchers decide what pitch they're throwing and where they are throwing it before they begin their delivery. Batters commit to the type and location of pitches they will swing at before the ball is thrown. Defensive players must predetermine where they're going to throw the ball if it's hit to them and how they're going to field it depending on where it's hit. Once that mind-set is in place, the body simply performs. Hitters, pitchers, and fielders can't think about where their feet, hands, elbows, hips, and so on should be while they're playing. Those thoughts are put to rest through repetitious training. If too much thought infiltrates the physical process, time is lost and execution will suffer.

Spending time perfecting the swing during the preseason can pay big dividends in game competition.

7

Perfect Practice Makes Improvement

We have all heard the cliché, "Practice makes perfect." Unfortunately, it doesn't quite work that way in baseball. First, it's integral that players practice the right way. If they do, they will improve. No question about it. But they will never be perfect. Not one major-league baseball player in the history of the game can honestly say that he perfected

Training the body through repetition allows players to react and execute immediately during the game.

LITTLE LEAGUE TRYOUTS

Tryouts can be a nervous ordeal for young players. Whether trying out to make a regular season team or a Little League all-star team, it's a tough situation for kids.

If there is one thing a coach or parent can do for a kid before tryouts, it's to not put any pressure on the player to make the team. Kids want to make the team badly enough on their own if they're willing to try out, so don't create any additional anxiety. Tell the player that regardless of the outcome, you're proud that he or she is taking a shot at making a team.

Practicing hitting, pitching, and/or fielding before tryouts helps build confidence and settle nerves. But a great suggestion you can tell players moments before tryouts is to make sure they hustle at all times. Coaches are drawn to kids who have enthusiasm and a great attitude. All coaches have seen, for example, a player botch a ground ball. It's part of the game. But if that player hustles after the miscue, retrieves the ball, and makes an accurate throw, it makes a positive impression on those observing.

Coaches are looking for good players, but they're also looking for good kids. A healthy, positive attitude can go a long way.

the game. Some have come closer than others, but there is always something that can be improved. There are always weaknesses that can be eliminated and strengths that can be embellished.

The rest of this section gives you drills to practice during the preseason for hitting, pitching, and fielding. These drills are designed to prepare players physically and mentally. As mentioned, drills and exercises are only beneficial to the player if they are being executed correctly. With that in mind, each topic (hitting, pitching, and fielding) is prefaced by an overview of the mechanics. Please read this part of the book carefully, then read it again, and always refer back to it in times of need. To guide youth players effectively, it's essential that a coach impart sound knowledge and present it in a fashion that is easily interpreted by kids. To do that, you must understand the components of the swing, pitching delivery, and fielding technique.

2

PRESEASON TRAINING FOR HITTING

No aspect of baseball is more fun than hitting, perhaps due to the challenge that it's the most difficult skill to master in all of sports. In order to succeed in something that is so complex, players must meticulously train their bodies to execute the proper move-

Putting the barrel of the bat on the ball consistently will send batting averages soaring.

ments instinctively (or without thought). These movements must be practiced over and over, so that eventually the roles of the stride, hips, and hands (among other things) become embedded in the player's muscle memory. The body simply reacts to the pitched ball, making the results dependent not on mechanics, but rather timing and execution.

The mistake young hitters make during preseason training is that they jump too far ahead, too quickly. They try to run before they can walk. Hitters are an impatient bunch and just want to jump in the batting cage and start taking hacks. This is how bad habits are born, and when those bad habits are practiced for weeks before entering the season, hitters set themselves up for a sagging batting average and a fragile state of mind.

When hitters take time off from baseball, considerable rust forms almost immediately. Body movements fall out of sync, bat speed diminishes, sharpened eyesight dulls, and the impenetrable confidence that was built from the previous season goes on sabbatical. The combination of these factors severely disrupts timing: when to stride, when to move the hands back, when to start the forward swing. Now, pitches that you're used to seeing your kids crush are missed, popped up, topped, or fouled off. The competitive zeal of the hitters then takes over and they begin to compensate their form and fundamentals in an effort to make solid contact. They start hacking at every pitch. Before long, they've made a mess of their swing and now lack the confidence to trust their own ability. Their next hitting session will be approached with self-doubt and discomfort.

The best way to start preseason training is to go back to the basics. Spend time retraining the hitters' bodies to execute the proper movements, to increase bat speed, to sharpen their focus on the baseball, and to build confidence. Be patient! Work on polishing the little things and reap the benefits of seeing big hits early in the spring.

Before discussing the necessary drills and practice regimen to prepare players, let's quickly review the mechanics of the swing. Consider this a refresher course, so that you can be sure to impart the correct information and be able to easily pick out mistakes if your students steer off course.

The Batting Stance

The two most important components of the batting stance are that it must be comfortable and workable. If hitters are not comfortable with their setup at the plate, confidence will suffer. With that, if the stance is not workable, you must interject and make an adjustment.

IMITATING BIG LEAGUERS CAN CAUSE BIG PROBLEMS

A lot of Little League hitters attempt to use batting stances of major-league players they see on television. It's safe to say that the stance used by New York Yankees shortstop Derek Jeter is imitated by more kids than any other major-league player. Watching players try to emulate their idols always brings a smile to onlookers, but it can hurt the players' chances of consistently hitting the ball. I'll use Jeter as an example.

Jeter holds his hands high in his stance, and when young players start their hands in this position, usually one of two things happens. The first is that they slice downward through the hitting zone. This descending swing causes them to contact the top of the ball (resulting in a chopper) or the bottom of the ball (resulting in a pop-up). Rarely is the ball struck in the middle.

The second is that they lower their hands as the pitch is thrown (to swing from a more comfortable position) before swinging the bat.

This makes them late to almost every pitch, especially fastballs on the inside part of the plate. Chopped balls and balls hit to the opposite field will be the typical result.

What Jeter fans fail to realize is that Number 2 starts with his hands high, but his hand position changes just before the pitch is delivered. As the pitcher swings his arm up, Jeter lowers his hands to his rear shoulder to get into a better position from which to swing the bat. At times, even Jeter is a little late bringing his hands down and is susceptible to inside fastballs. But Jeter is so good, he always seems to find a way to get the barrel on the ball and frustrate pitchers.

The lesson is that the hand position used by Jeter works for Derek Jeter. It may not be workable for an 11-year-old player. And the stance used by a successful 11-year-old player may not be workable for Derek Jeter. All players have their own individual style, swing, strengths, and weaknesses. Find what works best for each individual and go with it.

Hitters have all different types of stances that bring them success, but a traditional stance may be the best place to begin. Batters should stand with their feet placed slightly farther than shoulder-width apart. This puts them in a balanced position and allows them to utilize the strength of their lower body when swinging the bat. The weight rests on the balls of their feet—not on the toes or heels. Standing on the balls of the feet provides a sturdy foundation and places the hitter in an athletic position.

Because a hitter's stride should go directly toward the pitcher, the hitter should start from a square stance. The right and left feet are aligned and equidistant from home plate. A closed stance (front foot closer to home plate) and an open stance (front foot farther from home plate) can create problems in the stride foot landing in the desired square position.

The hitter should flex the knees (slightly) and shift more weight onto the rear leg—approximately 60 percent of his weight. The hands are held near the height of the rear shoulder and approximately three to five inches away from that shoulder. The shoulders are square to the pitcher and the head is turned so both eyes are facing the pitcher's mound.

Again, stances can vary from hitter to hitter. Hitters are of all different sizes, strengths, and abilities. The stance I've just described is standard, but each may differ slightly in some areas. Just remember, the stance must be comfortable and workable.

An example of a textbook stance. The feet are slightly farther than shoulder-width apart, squared up to the pitcher. The knees are bent, and hands held just off the rear shoulder.

Stride

When coaches compliment hitters, you hear comments like, "He's got great hands," or "He really fires his hips," or "His swing path is perfect." Rarely do you hear anyone comment on a hitter's stride, yet it is so critical to the swing. In fact, it's where most hitters' swings break down.

Two points to scrutinize when observing the stride are direction and weight distribution. Let's first discuss stride direction.

A square stance (as shown here) makes it simple to stride square, or directly toward the pitcher. This places the hitter in position to handle inside, middle, and outside strikes.

The hitter's stride should go directly toward the pitcher (or "square") on every single pitch. Period! This puts the body in position to distribute maximum power to the ball. It also gives hitters full plate coverage, meaning they're able to hit inside, middle, and outside strikes with authority.

From the stance position, the hitter takes a soft, short step approximately two to six inches in length. (Stride length varies due to stance width and player size.) The stride is generally taken as the pitcher releases the ball, but will vary on the arm strength of the pitcher. If the pitcher throws hard, the stride is taken sooner, and vice versa if the pitcher is a soft thrower. The stride touches down on the ball of the foot (never the heel) and remains closed. Again, each stride is directed straight toward the pitcher.

16

In the stance position (left), the hitter distributes more weight (60 percent) on his rear leg. As his stride foot lands (right), his weight remains loaded on his back side.

Striding open (away from home plate) is the most common mistake hitters make, especially early in the season. One problem this causes is that they then become susceptible to any pitches on the outer half of the plate. Smart pitchers will take notice that the hitter is stepping open and exploit this mistake by throwing pitches outside. The hitter's momentum is moving away from home plate with the stride, and the hitter will be forced to reach (weakly) for the pitch to make contact. In fact, all of the hitter's swings will pull away from home plate because the swing follows the direction of the stride. Anything but "middle-in" strikes will be hit weakly.

Striding closed (toward home plate) also causes problems. The hitter dives into the pitch and will be unable to fully rotate the hips. (Hip rotation is covered later in this section.) Outside strikes will be driven, but inside strikes will give this hitter fits.

Striding directly to the pitcher gives hitters their best chance of solid, powerful contact. Watch closely for stride direction as hitters take their swings.

Weight distribution is also a critical factor when the stride is taken. As the stride foot lands, the hitter's weight remains back. This keeps him in position to forcefully rotate the hips as he swings the bat and utilize the strength of the lower back, abdominal muscles, and legs. The weight shifts forward with the swing, thus maximizing the degree of power to and through the baseball. Keeping the weight back as the stride foot lands softly also keeps the head still and allows the eyes to track the pitch clearly.

A common mistake hitters make (especially in the preseason) is that they lunge forward with their stride and their weight shifts forward prematurely. This robs them of bat speed and power. When the weight transfers forward with the stride, the hips are unable to forcefully rotate and the batter swings with the upper body only. The lower body is all but eliminated from the swing.

When the hitter's weight drifts forward with the stride, it diminishes power and bat speed. Instead of firing the barrel with his hands and hips, the hitter is reduced to dragging the bat with his arms and shoulders.

Also, the head glides forward with a pronounced stride. This makes hitting extremely difficult. The eyes are unable to focus clearly on an object that is moving toward them. The ball will appear to be moving faster than it actually is, making the hitter jumpy, and most likely, late with the barrel. The stride should be soft and short so the head remains still.

18

Power Position

The position from which the hitter swings the bat is vital to performance. Each hitter's batting stance is a little different, but every good hitter gets into a good hitting position, or the "power position," before swinging the bat.

The power position is taken when the stride foot is down and the hands are moved back, just off the rear shoulder. As the pitch is released, the hitter moves the hands back to "load up" for power. In any sport in which you strike an object, there must be movement back to generate maximum power forward toward the object. A tennis player, golfer, and soccer player all have a backswing to initiate their forward movement. The movement back for a hitter is slight, but very important.

As the stride foot lands, the hands push back—not a shoulder-turn inward but a soft pushing of the hands. The movement is minimal. For example, if a hitter holds his hands just to the inside of the rear shoulder in the stance, the hands move back just past the outside of the rear shoulder. That's the extent of the movement. As

"Loading up" with the hands is a minimal but significant movement. The hands simply move back to start the swing from a more powerful position.

The hitter is set in the power position, poised to explode on the incoming pitch.

the hands reach the power position, they're now ready to explode forward to the ball.

A couple things to watch out for. The hands should not move upward, outward (away from the body), or wrap back behind the hitter's head. Any of these movements puts the hands in a position from which it is difficult to get the barrel to the ball in time consistently. The momentum and direction of the backward (or loading) movement should be as though a fishing line is attached to the back of the hitter's top hand, and someone tugs the line straight back.

Hips

When creating a visual image of a batter's swing, most people think about the hands, wrists, and arms firing the bat. The hips (or hip rotation) are as important to swinging the bat successfully as any part of the body.

Rotating the hips with the swing engages the lower half of the body and provides the hitter with increased bat speed and power. Some of the biggest muscle regions in the body—the lower back, the abdominal muscles, and the legs—are not used if the hips fail to rotate. In addition, as the hips rotate they clear a path for the hands to take a short, direct route to the ball, which produces a compact, powerful swing. Players can hit without hip rotation, but not with optimum power or consistency.

As the forward swing is initiated, the hips begin rotating
slightly ahead of the hands. Hip
rotation is fueled by the rear foot,
which pivots. On a pitch down the
middle of the strike zone, the hips
should face the pitcher in the finish position. The toes of the back
foot also face the pitcher's mound
and the rear leg forms an "L"
shape. The farther inside the
pitch, the more the hips rotate.
When the pitch is an outside
strike, the hips rotate to a lesser
degree.

Rotating the
hips (as
shown here)
allows the
hitter to
attack the ball
with his entire
body. Notice
the L shape in
the back leg,
indicating
excellent hip
rotation.

Remember, the hips must lead the hands in the swing. If hitters
rotate their hips after their hands have passed, the swing will be
long and at a reduced speed.

21

Swing

The path of the swing is very simple. It should begin at a slightly
downward angle, level off as it enters the hitting zone, stay level to
and through the baseball, and finally, ascend into the follow-
through. Having the bat level through the hitting zone (the point
at which the ball is struck) gives the hitter the best chance of solid
contact. If the bat is traveling slightly up or down, the barrel will
commonly catch the top or bottom of the ball.

To initiate the swing, the bottom hand begins to pull the bat forward and down toward the ball. As the handle of the bat nears the
midsection of the batter, the top-hand wrist unhinges and fires the

barrel of the bat to the ball. All batters should aspire to have a short, quick swing. Long, slow swings produce inconsistent and undesirable results.

As the swing makes contact with the ball, the hitter's hands should be in the palm-up, palm-down position. This means that the top hand palm is facing up and the bottom hand palm is facing down. The top hand should not be turned (or rolled) over at contact. The hands remain powerful and explosive in the palm-up, palm-down position. Hitters should maintain this position to and through the point of contact.

From the stance position, the hitter initiates his swing with his hands and hips. His hips begin to turn and his hands start down and forward to the ball (above right). As his hips continue to rotate, the bat moves on a downward path (next page, top left). The barrel never dips below the ball and levels off as it enters the hitting zone. The top hand then takes over and delivers the barrel to the ball.

At the point of contact (bottom left), the hands are in the palm-up, palm-down position, hips facing the pitcher. The arms are not quite at full extension. After contact is made, the barrel continues on a path through the ball before ascending into the finish position (bottom right).

The hitter must follow through completely on every swing to drive the ball with maximum power.

Follow-Through

The hitter's job is not completed when contact is made. The batter must finish the swing, or follow through, in order to maximize the strength of the swing.

Some hitters stop their swings prematurely, notably young hitters. To stop short of the follow-through, the hitter must actually slow the swing down before contact is made. This robs the swing of power.

Hitters have different follow-through positions depending on their stance (hand position) and swing path. Generally, the bat should finish just over the front shoulder. The finish should be slightly higher on high strikes and slightly lower on low strikes. Wherever the hands finish, the batter should always be in balance at the completion of the swing.

The Two-Week Preseason Training Plan for Hitters

In a perfect world, a baseball player has four to six weeks to prepare to hit, pitch, and/or field for the upcoming season. With the busy schedules of children and their heavy involvement in other activities, it's understandable that they're unable to commit that much time to preparation. With that in mind, I've created a two-week preseason program for young players to follow.

I'm going to warn you before I get started mapping out your first week for hitting: Do not fall victim to impatience! This week is

extremely important to building a foundation for a fur
sound swing. If you succumb to boredom and race f
hitter will spring leaks later down the road. Give wee
time and avoid future problems.

The first week is dedicated to making sure the batter is getting
in the correct position before starting the forward swing. Nearly
all flawed swings are faulty because of the position the hitter is in
before swinging the bat. Striding out, wrapping the hands, and pre-
mature weight shift are all examples of the hitter getting into a pre-
carious position before the forward swing is initiated.

Once the hitter gets into the proper position consistently, effective practice is nothing but repetitious swings. This trains the body
to execute properly and builds quickness and power using sound
mechanics. The best way to improve bat speed is to take swing after
swing after swing.

WEAR BATTING GLOVES DURING PRESEASON

Some batters like to wear batting gloves, while others like to feel
the handle of the bat in their bare hands. During preseason training,
hitters should wear batting gloves. If they don't, blisters will quickly
flare up and bring training to a halt. No batter, no matter how tough,
can adequately swing the bat with maximum force when the hands
develop blisters. It will then take several days for the blisters to heal
and shorten the time period to get ready for the season. Hitters
should wear batting gloves to start and then gradually wean themselves off of them. It's best to protect the hands that will produce
line drives and titanic blasts to the outfield.

Week One: Monday Through Saturday
(45 minutes per day)

Exercise 1   Power position reps—15 repetitions

Exercise 2   Slow-motion swings—15 swings

Exercise 3   Dry swings—15 middle strikes, 10 inside strikes, 10 outside strikes

Exercise 4   Tee work—20 middle strikes, 10 inside strikes, 10 outside strikes

Exercise 5   Soft toss—20 middle strikes, 10 high strikes, 10 low strikes

Exercise 6   Front toss—25 pitches to various locations

Power Position Reps

To swing the bat with power and consistency, the body must be in the proper position. Whether it's the position of the hands, stride foot, weight distribution, or shoulders, a swing can't be effectively executed if it starts astray from the power position.

In this drill, the hitter sets up in his customary stance and visualizes the pitcher in the windup. As the ball is about to be released, the stride foot moves forward and the hands push back to the power position. If this is executed correctly, the hitter will be in the following position:

The ball of the stride foot is touching the ground, heel slightly raised. The weight remains back, loaded on the rear leg. The head (and eyes) are still and have not moved forward. The hitter's hands have moved back just beyond the rear shoulder, and the front shoulder turns slightly inward. The bat is cocked slightly forward. As a reference point, if you're looking at a right-handed batter from the third-base side, the bat would be pointing to 11 o'clock; and a left-hander's bat would point to 1 o'clock from the first-base side.

Repeat this 15 times. This movement is what hitting instructors call "separation." The front foot moves forward as it strides, and

THE PITCHING MACHINE: A PRODUCER OF BAD HABITS

Hitting off pitching machines can have a purpose, but stay away from using them for the bulk of your training. Hitting off a machine can create bad habits.

The major problem with taking swings off pitching machines is that the hitters are unsure of when the ball will be delivered. They have some idea, but don't have the reassurance of seeing a person's armswing and then release point, which can be easily timed. What happens off the machine is the hitter will start to drift out onto the front foot in anticipation of the pitch. The weight of the body shifts forward prematurely, causing the head (and eyes) to move forward and forcing the batter to hit off of the front foot. From this position, the hitter will be unable to forcefully rotate the hips (because the weight is forward), and will swing the bat using only the upper body. If this swing is repeated time after time, drifting (or overstriding) will become habit—a very bad habit.

This most frequently occurs when hitting off pitching machines throwing at high speeds. Fathers are notorious for sticking their kids in high-speed cages with hopes of saying, "My kid hit off 75 miles per hour today." That may be true, but they probably compensated their natural mechanics to do so. The hitter's swing has now become infected and must be broken down and built back up.

The pitching machine is also artificial in that it generally throws the ball in the same place, at the same pace on every pitch. This is unrealistic and gives the hitter a false sense of security. When facing a pitcher, the batter does not know where the ball will be each time it's thrown. This forces the hitter to react to the location of the pitch, rather than having the comfort of knowing where the pitch will be every time off the machine. Parents often wonder why their children hit so well off the machine in cages, but fail to perform at the same level in games. Frankly, hitting is a lot easier if you know where the pitch will be every time. However, that is not the case in game competition.

Pitching machines are okay if they're delivering pitches at a slow speed. This keeps hitters from being jumpy in the batter's box in an attempt to meet a 75-mile-per-hour pitch that is spit out at them. With balls delivered at a very slow pace, hitters can focus on their swing mechanics and achieve repetitions. Other than that, stay away from machines.

the hands move back. It's from this position that hitters faithfully execute a quick, punishing swing.

Slow-Motion Swings

Swinging the bat takes approximately two- to three-tenths of a second. That's why creating muscle memory is so critical. If the hitter needs time to think about what movements the body needs to make, the ball will be past the batter and in the catcher's glove for a called strike. The purpose of the slow-motion swings is to learn and understand what the proper movements look and feel like. It provides the batter with a blueprint from which to pattern game-speed swings.

I'm going to walk you through a slow-motion swing and the sequence of movements to follow. Assume you're the batter and are looking out toward the pitcher. As the (imaginary) pitcher is about to release the ball, take a short, soft step toward the pitcher. As your front foot moves forward, your hands move back— "separation."

Just as you begin your forward swing, your hips begin to rotate by pivoting on your back foot. Your hands then begin moving forward on a direct line to the ball. (The knob of the bat actually points to the baseball in the early stages of the swing.) This initial movement is fueled by the lead arm (or bottom hand). As your hands begin to pass in front of your chest, the top hand begins to unhinge at the wrist to fire the barrel forward to the ball. The hips continue to rotate and clear a path for the hands to travel.

Slow-motion swings help hitters develop a feel for a mechanically sound swing.

As the barrel of the bat enters the hitting zone, it flattens out so it's traveling on a level path. This gives you the greatest chance of square contact. At the point of contact, the hands are in the palm-up, palm-down position. After contact is made, the hands continue in this position through the ball until extension is reached. Upon reaching extension, the top hand turns over into your follow-through. The bat finishes over the front shoulder.

At the completion of your swing, your front foot is slightly open, your hips face the pitcher, and your head is looking down at the point of contact. And perhaps most important, you are in a balanced position.

Hitters should take 15 slow-motion swings to familiarize their body with the proper movements. They're about to speed things up with dry swings, so take your time with this exercise. It's an excellent drill that focuses on form.

Dry Swings

The best way to increase bat speed is by taking repetitious swings. Now that sound fundamentals have been established through slow-motion swings, look to enhance the hitter's fast-twitch muscles by taking game-speed swings.

An important tip to keep in mind when game-speed swings are practiced is that maximum bat speed is accomplished only by staying relaxed and tension-free. Trying to swing too hard causes the muscles to contract, which robs the body of quickness. The hitter must focus on staying relaxed and being short and quick to the ball. That is when the bat will travel at its optimum speed.

For this drill, have the hitter visualize three separate pitch locations. The first 15 swings will concentrate on pitches thrown down the middle. The contact point should be at the top of home plate, and the hips should face the pitcher in the follow-through position.

The next 10 swings focus on attacking inside strikes. Two elements must change in order to accomplish this. First, the contact point is out in front of home plate. In order to put the barrel on an inside strike, the swing must start sooner to meet the ball earlier. If the ball travels too deep in the hitting zone, the hitter will get jammed. Second, the hips must fully rotate. Upon the swing's completion, the hips should face the shortstop for right-handed hitters and the second-base position for left-handed hitters. The hips must rotate this far to clear a path for the hands to stay through the ball in front of home plate.

The final 10 swings address outside strikes. The adjustments to driving outside strikes are the exact opposite of inside strikes. The hitter must allow the ball to travel deeper in the hitting zone

Dry swings are great for developing muscle memory, and hitters can practice them anywhere.

30

and start the swing later. The contact point is toward the back of home plate. In addition, the hips should quiet, rotating slightly so they finish facing the opposite-field middle infielder.

Attacking the outside strike out in front of home plate will produce hits devoid of power. Hitters will reach for the pitch and strike the ball in a compromising (less powerful) position. Firing the hips open will pull the body away from the ball, most commonly causing the barrel to drag and weakly catch the bottom of the ball.

The bat is to be delivered aggressively with each swing, but check to make sure balance is maintained. If the hitter is falling forward (toward home plate) or backward (away from home plate), the swing is flawed and needs fine-tuning.

Tee Work

There is no hitting tool more important to developing proper mechanics than the batting tee. Coaches and parents can buy all the crazy contraptions in the world, but nothing can take the place of taking swings off the tee. That is why it has been used by hitters for nearly 100 years.

Here is why the batting tee is so useful to perfecting the swing. By placing the ball on a tee, two major variables are eliminated from the hitters' focus: timing and pitch location. The ball just sits there, which allows the hitters to concentrate on executing the correct movements rather than shifting their attention to the speed of the pitch and where it's located. If hitters, for example, fall to their heels every time they take their stride, it's very difficult for them to concentrate on eliminating that bad habit while a ball is being pitched to them. With the ball sitting on the tee, they can more easily focus on staying balanced on the balls of their feet throughout the swing.

Don't try to correct mechanics by throwing pitch after pitch after pitch. The hitter will progress (if at all) at a snail's pace, and both

The photo on the left illustrates the proper positioning when hitting off a batting tee. The hitter stands back far enough to achieve extension through the swing. A common mistake young hitters make is that they stand too close to the plate (right) and restrict their swing.

of you will become frustrated. Rebuild the mechanics from the tee and then gradually progress to batting practice.

When batters hit off the tee, make sure they're standing in the correct position. The tendency is to stand too far forward (north to south) and not allow for extension through the ball. On middle strikes, the stem of the tee should be positioned so that the contact point is at the top of home plate.

The batters should take 20 swings with the tee set up for pitches down the middle. Give the hitters a visual image that there is a second ball directly behind the ball on the tee and that their swing should drive through both baseballs. This promotes hitting through the ball and stops hitters from prematurely rolling the wrists or cutting the swing short.

The batting tee is one of the best tools for swing mechanics.

Move the tee forward and in toward the hitter to practice inside strikes (10 swings). As explained in the dry-swings drill, contact is made out in front of home plate on inside strikes. The hitter should focus on firing the hips to achieve full rotation.

Move the tee back and away from the hitter to practice outside strikes (10 swings). Contact is made near the back and outside portion of the plate for these pitches. Hip rotation is minimal, and the hitter must make sure the top hand keeps the barrel up to strike the ball. The tendency is to let the barrel dip when attacking outside strikes.

Soft Toss

Another great drill for establishing a solid foundation of fundamentals is soft toss. Because the ball is tossed from a very short distance, batters can remain focused on their swing while hitting a moving ball.

If tossing to a right-handed batter, the tosser sets up to the right, and slightly in front of, the hitter. The ball is firmly tossed underhand to the batter's front hip. The hitter should start the stride and move the hands back as the ball is released. The hitter's objective is to hit line drives back through the middle for the first 20 swings.

Next, toss balls to the upper part of the strike zone (above the belt). This forces the hitters to practice hitting high strikes. They must raise their hands before the swing to deliver the barrel on a level path. Hitters make the mistake of swinging up at high strikes and commonly produce pop-ups, foul balls, and swings and misses. The correct method is to raise the hands, fire the barrel on a level plane with the pitch, and then stay through the ball on that plane. Toss the batter 10 consecutive high strikes.

Hitters attack low strikes by using their legs. The rear leg must collapse slightly as the hitter rotates (or pivots on the back foot) to

Vary the height of each toss so hitters can expand their vertical hitting zone.

lower the plane of the swing. Hitters commonly drop the barrel of the bat to the ball when the pitch is down but often fail to achieve solid contact. The batter must use his legs to get the bat on a level plane with the pitch. Also, the follow-through on this swing is lower. If the hitter rises up and out of the swing too quickly to finish the swing high, the bat will catch the top of the ball and produce a chopper. Toss 10 balls low in the strike zone to practice this swing.

Front Toss

This drill requires an L-screen, or at least something that the tosser can stand behind. Using a customary L-screen, turn the screen around so that the straight edge is on the throwing side. From approximately 15 to 25 feet, toss balls underhand to the hitter from straight ahead. Right after the ball is released, step behind the screen for protection from batted balls.

This is one of the best exercises for hitters during any part of the season. It allows the batter to see balls from the front and the feeder to accurately deliver balls in varying locations—middle, inside, outside, high, and low. Because the ball is thrown underhand, hitters can concentrate on their technique and feel how powerfully the ball leaves the bat when the body functions properly.

During preseason, hitters take 25 swings per day. Deliver pitches to different parts of the strike zone so they're forced to react to varying locations. Look to see if any particular pitch locations give the hitter trouble. If so, and if time permits, go a second round and work toward improving the weakness.

While these drills are designed to develop a good swing, they are also building something that's even more important to hitters. By taking swing after swing and hitting balls off the barrel of the bat during these simple exercises, hitters build confidence. They become comfortable with their stance, hand position, stride, and so on, and the body starts to react with greater authority.

Think of the alternative. A kid goes in the cage and swings at 75 pitches thrown by a coach or parent. Half of those pitches will most likely be thrown out of the strike zone. Out of frustration or sheer impatience, the hitter will begin practicing swinging at bad pitches. Because the hitter has not hit in some time, his timing will be off. So of the 30 to 35 pitches that are strikes, many balls will be missed or poorly struck due to a flawed sense of timing. Another bag of balls will be missed or mishit because of poor mechanics. Frustration will begin to set in and the hitter will respond by either over-swinging or slowing down the swing with hopes of just making contact. Too much or too little effort adversely affects swing mechanics.

So out of that session, maybe 8 to 10 balls are hit really well; hardly a workout that a young hitter can walk away from brimming with confidence. The swing, and the belief in oneself, has to be built from the ground up regardless of age or talent. Do the drills religiously, monitor the progress, and then move to live pitching when the hitter is ready.

Week Two: Monday Through Saturday

Exercise 1 Dry swings—10 middle strikes, 10 inside strikes, 10 outside strikes

Exercise 2 Tee work—10 middle strikes, 10 inside strikes, 10 outside strikes

Exercise 3 Soft toss, long—20 middle strikes, 10 high strikes, 10 low strikes

Exercise 4 Front toss—20 pitches

Exercise 5 Short batting practice (BP)—20 pitches

Exercise 6 Batting practice—15 pitches

Exercise 7 Game at-bats—10 at-bats

During the second week of training, the focus remains on the fundamentals of the swing. What's most important is that the hitter learns to swing the bat correctly. A good swing takes precedence over great results. It's better that the batter swings the bat right and fouls pitches off (or even misses) rather than compensating the mechanics just to put the bat on the ball. Improper mechanics will eventually haunt the hitter later in the season and later in his career. Concentrate on doing it right and the results will follow.

In this second week, live throwing has been added to the mix. With little time before tryouts, it's essential that hitters see pitches thrown to them to build comfort at the plate. However, that does not mean to start firing pitches from 46 feet. Gradually ease the hitter into live swings by starting with short-distance batting practice and then slowly backing up.

Dry Swings

Don't skip it! Start each session by taking 10 swings on pitches down the middle, 10 inside strikes, followed by 10 outside strikes. The batters will be forced to concentrate on their swing and continue to train mind and body how to react differently to varying pitch locations. Make sure the hitters finish in a balanced position after each swing.

Tee Work

Next, take 30 swings off the tee—10 middle, 10 outside, 10 inside. Remember to move the tee forward and in for inside strikes, back and away for outside strikes. Pay attention to how the ball is coming off the hitters' bat and their finish position. Watch to ensure the hitters are rotating their hips with each swing and that the swing

HOW HARD SHOULD I THROW IN BATTING PRACTICE?

Pitch velocity is not as important as most adults assume, especially during the preseason. Throwing balls at a moderate pace accomplishes several things for the batter. (1) Most hitters have some degree of fear in preseason because they haven't seen balls thrown in their direction in quite some time. That's human instinct. When something is thrown in our direction, the normal reaction is to get out of the way. That element of fear is minimized when pitches are thrown at medium speed—the batter feels less danger and is thus encouraged to stride square. The number one mechanical flaw in the preseason is that hitters stride open or away from the pitch. (2) The pitcher will throw more strikes, which makes the batting-practice sessions more productive. Unleashing pitches at maximum velocity diminishes accuracy. Throw the ball at a firm pace so the hitter gets more swings. (3) Hitters will strike more balls off the barrel of the bat when facing pitches at medium speed. The worst-case scenario would be for the hitters to hit one out of every 10 or 20 pitches solid. Now, their confidence dives into a tailspin. The purpose of batting practice is to build confidence, not create self-doubt.

One last point: Throwing at medium speed from a shortened distance actually simulates the reaction time a batter has in a game. Think about it. If a ball is thrown 40 miles per hour from 30 feet, it takes roughly the same amount of time to reach the hitter as does a 55-miles-per-hour pitch from 46 feet. The batter has the same amount of time to react to the pitch. However, there will be less fear from the hitter, more strikes thrown by the pitcher, and more productive swings overall.

is compact and powerful. Balls should be struck off the barrel with a high percentage of consistency.

Soft Toss, Long

From the traditional soft-toss position, have the hitters hit balls the length of the batting cage, or if you're outside, out onto the field. This allows you to observe the flight of the ball. Ball flight can indicate whether the ball is struck correctly or incorrectly. Golfers pay strict attention to their ball flight and can determine what they're doing wrong mechanically just by seeing how the ball carries off the club.

A typical example of this in baseball is seeing balls hook in mid-flight. This type of ball flight indicates one of a few things. (1) The hitter is getting around the ball with the swing and contacting the outside of the ball. (2) The hitter's front shoulder is pulling out prematurely. (3) The hitter's top hand is rolling over prematurely. Instead of being in the palm-up, palm-down position at and through contact, the top hand begins to roll into the follow-through as the ball is struck.

Toss 20 pitches to the middle of the strike zone, 10 high strikes and 10 low strikes. The hitter should produce a level swing on each toss, regardless of its height. Pay attention to the flight of the ball to assure it's being hit with sound mechanics.

Front Toss

From behind an L-screen, toss middle, inside, and outside strikes. The hitters should approach each pitch as if they're going to hit a line drive back through the middle, then react to the pitch location. If a specific pitch location is giving a hitter trouble (for example, low and outside strikes), spend additional time focusing on that pitch.

Short Batting Practice (BP)

Stand behind an L-screen approximately 30 feet from the hitter. Throw firm pitches, reminding the hitter to swing only at strikes. The batter should attempt to hit the first five pitches to the opposite field. This forces the hitter to see the ball long and establish a sense of timing. Commonly, young hitters attempt to crush every pitch from the get-go and fail to have a productive session.

Batting Practice (BP)

From regulation distance (or just short of regulation), throw a round of batting practice. The hitter should take 15 swings to get familiar with timing pitches from that distance. Again, demand that the batter hit the first five balls to the opposite field.

Game At-Bats (10 At-Bats)

This round places the hitter in a game situation. Counts are kept just as if the batter were in competition. If the first pitch is a ball, the count is 1-0. If the next pitch is fouled off, the count goes to 1-1.

The purpose of this exercise is to polish the hitter's approach and how it changes in different counts. Early or ahead in the count, the hitter should look for pitches he can handle well. For example, on a 2-0 count the hitter is at an advantage and can be more selective and look for pitches that he likes. Some hitters like pitches that are inside. If that is the case, the hitter should swing only at pitches on the inside part of the plate.

Behind in the count, the approach differs. If the count is 1-2, the batter must expand the strike zone and protect home plate. He can no longer choose pitches in the strike zone on which to swing the bat; he must swing or be called out on strikes.

Hitters always enjoy this drill. Judge whether fair-hit balls are hits or outs. Pitches should be thrown at (or just short of) regulation distance.

BATTING PRACTICE
FOR PEE WEE PLAYERS

A good idea for parents and coaches who throw batting practice to pee wee–aged players is to throw from one knee. This lowers the height of your release point and more accurately simulates the ball flight of a pitch thrown by a player the child's age.

Drop to one knee when tossing batting practice to pee wee Little Leaguers.

When adults stand up and throw to small children, the children are looking up and commonly tilt their shoulders upward to hit a pitch traveling down at them. Right then and there, a bad habit is formed. They'll develop an uppercut because their rear shoulder is lower than their front shoulder. Get down on their level, so their shoulders (and swing) can stay level.

Game at-bats include additional variables like timing, pitch location, pitch selection, and count hitting.

The hitters are now in good shape for upcoming tryouts and the season's beginning. They have established a solid foundation of mechanics, understand their strengths and weaknesses at the plate, have developed a sense of timing, and know when to look for their pitch and when to protect the plate. More important, the batters are confident. They have done their homework and prepared diligently for the upcoming season.

While the hitters have prepared, their work is not completed. Hitting is a craft that is never perfected. Continue with these exercises and drills to keep the hitters sharp and to improve their prowess at the plate throughout the season.

3

PRESEASON TRAINING FOR PITCHING

Not many would argue that pitching is the most critical position on the baseball field. When two quality pitchers oppose each other, generally, a quality game follows. Preseason preparation for pitchers is extremely important. Like hitters, learning the proper mechanics through repetitious training is the only way to achieve consistent results. The additional factor is, however, that pitchers must condition their arms to be ready for competitive play.

There are plenty of kids out there who have "good arms." Early in their careers, they can rely on their ability to throw the baseball at better-than-average speed to get batters out. But those days will be short-lived. Throwers fall back to the middle of the pack, while pitchers will begin to rise to the top. There are several

Good pitching will defeat good hitting at every level of play.

differences between a thrower and a pitcher, but the most significant difference is proper throwing mechanics. Good mechanics allow the pitcher to maximize pitch velocity, throw the baseball accurately for consistent command of the strike zone, and reduce the chances of arm soreness and injury.

The Pitching Mechanics

It's important to review the pitching fundamentals before initiating a pitching program. My good friend Randy Voorhees, author of *Coaching the Little League Pitcher*, has broken the pitching delivery into four stages: knee raise and foot press; ball separation and glide step; landing, forward armswing, glove-arm pull; and extension and finish. Each stage will be briefly described before discussing the preseason program. To keep the text simple to follow, I will put you (the reader) in the body of the pitcher.

Stage One: Knee Raise and Foot Press

The delivery from the set position begins with a simple raise of the stride-leg knee. Raise your knee up to your belt with your foot hanging directly below. The toes of your foot should point down as it hangs. As you raise your knee, rotate slightly inward so that the catcher can barely see your rear pocket. (Don't go so far the catcher can see the numbers on your jersey.) Flex your post (or standing) leg slightly, keeping your hands in front of your chest and eyes on the target.

After you've concluded your knee raise, press your stride foot back down toward the ground. Do not swing it out and forward toward home plate. This leads to "rushing out," one of the most common flaws made by pitchers. The lower body gets out in front of the upper body and pitching arm, thus decreasing velocity and command. Take the time to press back down before gliding out into the stride.

THE SET POSITION

Young pitchers should go out of their way to keep things simple. Long-winded windups with quirky movements disrupt pitchers' timing and can cause them to fall off balance. This puts them in a poor position to deliver the ball, thus diminishing velocity and especially accuracy. Keep it basic and minimize the chances of a flawed delivery.

A simple delivery makes it easier for the pitcher to maintain balance. From the set position, the pitcher just raises his knee to initiate the windup.

The set position is easy to establish. The pitcher places the outside of the pivot foot against the pitching rubber and the stride foot shoulder-width distance away in the direction of home plate. The ball is held in the glove directly in front of the chest and all points on the glove side of the body are closed to the target. Body weight is evenly distributed between the two feet as the pitcher looks directly over the lead shoulder at the target. Starting the delivery only entails a simple knee raise.

The knee is raised up, and then presses straight back down.

46

Stage Two: Ball Separation and Glide Step

After you have completed your foot press, glide toward the target with your stride leg. As you begin your glide, remove the ball from your glove and swing it down, back, and up into throwing position. The throwing position is often called the "power" position. In this position, the throwing-arm elbow is at shoulder height. It is flexed and free of tension. The ball is faced out toward center field. Many coaches tell their pitchers to "show the ball to the center fielder." Extend your glove arm down the target line until it's nearly shoulder-height.

After you have pressed your stride foot down, glide toward home plate with your stride leg. The glide step is a controlled fall toward home plate. All points on your front side (shoulder, hip, knee, foot) remain closed to the target during the glide step.

It is essential that you initiate the glide step with the lower half of your body. Do not fall forward with your upper body—stay tall.

The length of your stride depends on your height. Roughly, the glide step should be 80 to 90 percent of body height. Understriding produces pitches that are low, and overstriding results in pitches up in or high out of the strike zone.

Stage Three: Landing, Forward Armswing, Glove-Arm Pull

At the completion of your glide step, your stride foot lands softly on the ground. Land flat-footed or on the ball of your foot, but never the heel. Touching down on your heel can cause you to lose balance.

The direction of your stride is extremely important. Your foot should land directly on the target line or slightly to the right (if you're a right-handed pitcher). This keeps your body aligned with

As the stride foot lands, the glove arm extends toward the target and the throwing arm swings up toward the power position.

the target and closed, poised to explode with your entire body as the pitching arm sets to accelerate forward.

Once the stride foot hits the ground, your throwing arm and hand move forward toward the target. Your elbow remains at least as high as your shoulder until no earlier than the release of the pitch. At release, your fingers are behind and over the baseball. Think about throwing the ball on a downward angle (or downhill) to accomplish this. As you release (the release point), your arm should continue to accelerate. Your point of release should remain consistent with every pitch.

As you're moving your throwing arm forward, pull your glove arm back in toward your body. Turn the fingers of the glove toward the sky and pull your elbow in toward your side. The action should

The glove arm pulls into the midsection as the throwing arm fires forward to deliver the ball.

feel almost as if you're elbowing someone behind you. This pulling action complements the pulling action of your throwing side. It helps generate greater arm speed (and pitch velocity) and also takes pressure off your throwing-arm side.

Stage Four: Extension and Finish

After the pitch is released, extend your throwing arm down and across the target line until you finish with your hand across the mid-to-lower part of your stride leg. Extending through your pitch will help to ensure that you do not decelerate your arm prematurely. This forceful momentum also pulls your entire body into the pitch.

How a pitcher finishes depends on many different factors: the size of the pitcher, the pitching style, and also the point of release. In general, your pivot foot should finish past the stride foot and on (or close to) the target line. Your upper body should be bent slightly forward, with your throwing arm draped across the target line and over the stride-leg knee. Your head should be facing home plate, eyes still focused on the target.

Note: What has been outlined is a blueprint for perfect pitching mechanics. Young pitchers should make every attempt to model their delivery along these guide-lines, however, it is possible to stray from perfect form and still be an effective pitcher. There are many major-league pitchers who have mechanical flaws, but have obviously experienced enough success to compete in the big leagues. If a young pitcher has success on the mound while showcasing an unorthodox deliv-ery, it's important to ask yourself a few questions.

The arm swings down and across the plant leg, eyes on the target to finish the pitch.

- Does the pitcher appear to be free and easy (free of strain and tension) throughout the pitching motion?
- Does the pitcher have consistent command of his pitches?
- Is the velocity of the pitches about what you would expect from the pitcher?
- Is the pitcher free of soreness?

If the answer is yes to these questions, it might be best to leave the pitcher alone. As mentioned, many great pitchers have possessed mechanical glitches in their delivery. However, one last important question needs to be asked. Will the mistake in the pitching motion catch up to the pitcher at higher levels of play? In other words, is the pitcher getting away with something now that will be exposed in the future? That may be a difficult question to answer, but one that should be pondered.

A four-seam fastball grip is used to maximize carry and velocity.

A two-seam fastball grip adds movement to the pitch.

DO I TEACH A LITTLE LEAGUE PITCHER TO THROW A BREAKING BALL?

This question has plagued Little League parents and coaches for years and will continue to be a topic of controversy. If taught correctly and executed properly, breaking balls can be thrown without risk of injury. But when it's not taught the right way, or if the pitcher fails to interpret the instruction the way it's imparted, throwing a breaking pitch can cause arm problems.

The best path to take is to teach the change-up. It serves as an off-speed pitch that frustrates and confuses hitters. Throwing it requires the same arm action as a fastball, but with a modified grip. This makes it nearly impossible for hitters to detect and offers no risk of injury to the pitcher.

The change-up should be the second pitch of every young pitcher. Any good hitter will tell you that a pitcher with a good change-up is devastating to face.

51

The Two-Week Preseason Training Plan for Pitchers

If you asked Little League pitchers what they need to do leading up to the baseball season to have success on the mound, they would probably say, "I've got to get my arm ready." There is truth to that, but preseason training for pitchers should not be isolated to their throwing arm. The lower half of the body is equally important during the conditioning stages. Pitchers use their legs, buttocks, torso, and abdominal muscles when throwing the baseball. Relying solely on arm strength will result in short stints on the hill, and even worse, injury. Distance and short-interval running are critical elements to conditioning the body for pitching.

Obviously, the pitching arm must be conditioned as well. There are no hidden secrets in how to build arm strength and prepare the arm for the season. Simply put, the pitcher has to throw. What is critical is that the throwing is performed properly and that it is controlled. Going in the backyard and throwing 75 pitches from 46 feet on day one is not a good idea. Throwing-form drills, short-distance pitching, and limited sets from the mound allow pitchers to gradually learn the proper mechanics, build arm strength, command their pitches, and develop overall confidence. Below are both weeks one and two presented in succession. Descriptions of all the drills and exercises follow. To better understand each drill and how they're executed, first try them yourself.

Week One: Monday Through Saturday

Monday	One-knee drill, balance and glide drill, throw and finish drill, play catch from 46 feet, run distance
Tuesday	One-knee drill, balance and glide drill, throw and finish drill, long toss, sprints
Wednesday	One-knee drill, balance and glide drill, throw from the mound 40 pitches, run distance
Thursday	One-knee drill, balance and glide drill, throw and finish drill, play catch from 46 feet with change-up grip, pitcher fielding practice (PFPs)
Friday	One-knee drill, balance and glide drill, throw and finish drill, long toss, sprints, interval running
Saturday	One-knee drill, balance and glide drill, pitch from the mound 40 pitches, run distance

Week Two: Monday Through Saturday

Monday	One-knee drill, balance and glide drill, throw and finish drill, throw 25 flat-ground pitches, sprints, interval running
Tuesday	One-knee drill, balance and glide drill, throw and finish drill, long toss, PFPs
Wednesday	One-knee drill, balance and glide drill, throw from the mound 50 pitches, run distance
Thursday	One-knee drill, balance and glide drill, throw and finish drill, catch from 46 feet, sprints, interval running
Friday	One-knee drill, balance and glide drill, long toss, sprints, PFPs
Saturday	One-knee drill, balance and glide drill, throw off mound 60 pitches, run distance

Throwing Drills

One-Knee Drill

Place the knee of your post leg (right knee for a right-handed pitcher) on the ground with your stride foot flat on the ground for balance. Hold your glove directly in front of your chest with your hand holding the ball in your glove. Rotate your shoulders and separate into the power position. Now deliver the pitch, making sure to extend your throwing arm down and across your stride leg and to pull your glove arm down and into your side. From a distance of approximately 20 feet, the pitcher should throw 15 to 20 balls during this drill.

Balance and Glide Drill

Balance on your post leg with the stride leg in the perfect lift position (foot hanging directly under the knee). Press your stride foot

The one-knee drill

down and back up twice without touching the ground, then press it down a third time, glide down the target line, and deliver the pitch. From a distance of approximately 30 feet, the pitcher should throw 10 to 15 balls during this drill.

The balance and glide drill

Throw and Finish Drill

Set up in the power position with your feet slightly more than shoulder-width apart. You're simulating the position in which you land during the delivery. Throw the ball without moving your stride foot forward, making sure you get maximum arm extension and good glove-side pull, and pivoting on your stride foot. Check your finish position to make sure your arm ends up across your post leg. From a distance of approximately 30 feet, throw 10 to 15 balls during this drill.

Playing Catch (46 feet)

With your focus on executing proper throwing mechanics, play catch with your partner from 46 feet (the distance from the pitching rubber to home plate). Do not "max out" on your throws, but rather throw at about 75 percent effort. Concentrate on getting into the power position, staying balanced throughout your delivery, and finishing your pitches.

Instead of simply throwing to a general area, pick isolated targets on your partner to work on commanding your throws. For example, aim five throws at the middle of your partner's chest. Next, throw five balls at the right thigh of your partner. Throw balls to a specific target to condition your level of concentration and build confidence in controlling your pitches. Throw 15 to 25 balls during this drill.

Playing Catch (from 46 feet with change-up grip)

Repeat the same drill that is written above, but use your change-up grip every time you throw the ball. A basic change-up is thrown with the exact same delivery as a fastball, only the grip is altered. To throw a four-seam circle change-up, place the pads of your middle and ring fingers across the seam of the ball and approximately one inch apart. Hold the ball deep in these fingers, but don't squeeze

The circle change-up grip. There are several change-up grips that are effective. The pitcher must find a grip that feels comfortable, and play catch with it to increase comfort.

it. Slide your pinky finger underneath the ball. Move your thumb to the inside of the baseball and bend your index finger down to meet your thumb, forming a circle.

Playing catch with a change-up grip is the best way for pitchers to become comfortable throwing that pitch. There is no additional strain on the arm when it's thrown, but when thrown correctly, it can cause a lot of stress in the mind of the batter.

Long Toss
Long toss is a drill used for building arm strength. Begin playing catch from approximately 40 feet and back up 5 feet every five throws. Continue moving back until you reach 70 feet. Be sure to maintain proper mechanics when throwing. Do not tilt your shoulders upward in an effort to launch the ball farther. During the lat-

ter stages of this drill, do not unleash high, arcing throws. Keep the ball on a straight line. If you can no longer reach your partner in the air, do so on one bounce.

Throwing from the Mound

The purpose of throwing from the mound is to establish sound mechanics (off the pitching mound), develop command of your pitches, and build arm strength. Throw your pitches at about 85 percent effort. First, establish rhythm and focus on staying balanced throughout your delivery. For the first 10 pitches, simply locate the ball in the strike zone. From there, look to command your pitches to specific areas of the strike zone—in, out, up, and down.

Conditioning Drills

Running Distance

Throwing a lot of pitches during a game is taxing on the pitchers' arms, but even more so on their legs. Pitchers lose control of the strike zone late in the game because their legs wear out, which forces them to exert more effort with their arm. This can lead to soreness and injury. Distance running keeps pitchers' legs strong and provides them with greater endurance.

The length of the distance depends on the age and physical maturity of the pitcher. Anywhere from a half mile to a mile is a good starting point. Whatever starting distance is selected, increase it each time out.

Sprinting

Sprint work is essential because it helps pitchers with those quick bursts of power that they need when pitching. Begin with 30-yard sprints and extend to 40 to 50 yards as players gain strength and endurance. Allow players some time between sprints for recovery.

Interval Running

Interval running alternates between slow jogging and sprinting. Most pitchers do this by jogging from one foul pole in the outfield to the other foul pole and then sprinting back. When starting out, the players should try to go back and forth between foul poles three to five times. As the players gain strength and endurance, increase the length of the interval workout.

Pitcher Fielding Practice (PFP) Drills

Comebackers

The pitcher simulates the delivery of the pitch, then fields a ground ball hit by the coach. He fields the ball and then throws to a designated base. Vary the bases the pitcher throws to so he becomes comfortable throwing to each base (first, second, third, and home). Take the time to preach footwork before throwing, making sure that the feet are aligned to the base to which the pitcher is throwing.

Practicing comebackers to the mound is a form of conditioning, but is also helpful for when the situation arises in a game.

Bunt Coverage

Pitchers must practice getting off the mound and fielding bunts. It's a part of the game that is not practiced nearly enough. Roll (or bunt) balls directly back to the pitcher, to the third-base side, and to the first-base side. After the pitcher simulates a pitch, drop down a bunt and then call out the base the ball should be thrown to.

Covering First

The pitcher simulates a pitch, the coach hits a ground ball to the first baseman, and the pitcher runs over to cover first. Any time a ground ball takes a first baseman to his right, it's essential that the pitcher run over to cover the bag. Practice this 10 times per session.

4

PRESEASON TRAINING FOR FIELDING

This may sound a little backward, but the primary job of the pitcher is to make the batter hit the ball. Any time the ball is put into play, it provides an opportunity to record an out. With that in mind, if the players on a Little League baseball team can catch the ball and throw it accurately, they will win their share of games—plain and simple. So much emphasis is placed on hitting and pitching that team defense is typically overlooked. Fielding may not possess the glamour and individual attention that hitting and pitching boast, but it is of equal (and sometimes more) importance. Defense can make or break a team.

Throwing

Throwing the ball correctly improves accuracy, maximizes the speed of throws, and diminishes the chance of arm soreness and injury. From a competitive standpoint, throwing the ball efficiently from one teammate to another is a way of recording outs. Outs are what get you off the field and in to hit.

Good defense will produce scores of victories in Little League baseball.

The correct way to grip the ball is across the seams, making sure to keep the fingers on top of the ball. The player steps directly toward the target and keeps the lead shoulder closed (using it as sort of a gun sight). The throwing arm swings down and back and up in a fluent motion. As the arm is raised up, the ball faces directly away from the target. The player's throwing arm continues to swing up to the overhand position, the glove arm then pulls in toward the body and the throwing arm shoulder begins to externally rotate. The throwing arm accelerates forward and the ball is released at the one o'clock or two o'clock position. The arm continues forward and then down and across the body and finishes across the opposite-side leg (left leg for a right-handed thrower and vice versa).

The distance of the throw dictates the length of the arm swing. Outfielders employ a longer backswing because their throws generally have to travel a greater distance. Infielders have shorter throws and also have less time to release the ball, so a shorter arm-swing is required.

Fielding Ground Balls

When Little League players get into the proper position, they generally field ground balls consistently. It's when their body is in a poor position that the percentages decline. Players must practice the proper position repeatedly before attempting to field batted balls.

First, fielders must position their feet far apart to widen their base. This allows them to get low to the ground and reach for the ball. The distance the feet are spread apart varies on the size of the player, but the feet should be well outside shoulder-width. At all times, the weight of the body is on the balls of the feet. A slight lean forward eliminates the prospect of falling back on the heels when fielding—an absolute no-no.

In order to reach for the ball, players must bend at the knees to lower their rear end. The most common mistake Little League players make is that they bend at the waist. Bending at the knees and getting the rear end down provides the best setup from which to field ground balls. It enables fielders to reach for the ball and see it enter the glove. Fielding the ball back (underneath the body) creates the risk of losing sight of the ball and fielding back on the heels.

Infielders should be set in the ready position on every pitch.

Whenever possible, the ball is fielded in the center of the body.

63

GOBBLING UP GROUNDERS

Players should be taught to follow five steps in fielding grounders:

1. Move your feet so the ball is fielded in the middle of your body.
2. Spread your feet apart to widen your base.
3. Bend at the knees and lower the rear end.
4. Reach for the ball with two hands.
5. Look the ball into the glove and secure it with two hands.

This aligns the eyes with the ball and keeps the body behind the ball should it take a bad hop. The glove arm extends out holding the glove wide open. The glove should be held like a shovel as the ball is fielded. The fingers rest on the ground, but the back of the glove is slightly raised off the ground. The throwing hand is held above the glove, poised to secure the ball once it has entered the mitt.

Instruct infielders to think of the fielding position in terms of a triangle. The imaginary line drawn between their feet represents the base of the triangle, and the glove (reaching out for the ball) rests at the apex (or top) of the triangle. Fielders should try to create this triangle each time they field the ball. And remember, bend at the knees and reach!

Players should lower the rear end and reach for the ball with two hands when fielding a routine ground ball, and should center the ball in the middle of the body and keep their balance leaning slightly forward.

Fielding Fly Balls

When a ball leaves the bat airborne in a Little League baseball game, the reactions on the faces of parents and coaches are often entertaining. Everyone holds their collective breath as the ball reaches its peak and then falls from the sky. If you're coaching a Little League team that can catch fly balls, you're in good shape. A team that has trouble catching balls out of the air is in trouble.

Why do youth players have so much difficulty catching fly balls? Is the technique that complex? No it isn't; however, there are two factors that play a much greater role than technique: fear and judgment.

When something falls out of the sky, people are taught to run for cover. In baseball, kids are asked to position themselves so they stand directly under the falling object. To eliminate that instinctual fear, players must be eased into it through repetition. Toss balls underhand from short distances and gradually increase the height. Once a degree of comfort has been reached, begin to throw overhand pop-ups before eventually hitting balls off the bat.

The proper technique is simple. The fingers of the glove should be pointed toward the sky. The glove is held to the right or left of the outfielder's head, depending on comfort and to what side the ball is hit. Make sure players do not block their eyes with their glove. The eyes are their protector and mustn't be obstructed. The eyes follow the ball all the way down and into the glove's pocket. Fly balls are always caught with two hands, unless reaching for the ball on the run.

At an early age, players should be trained to catch the ball over their throwing shoulder whenever possible. This places them in position to catch, reach in their glove for the ball, and quickly throw it back to the infield. This is an advanced skill for Little League players, but if they get into the habit early, it's one less thing they'll have to learn as they progress.

On balls that players must run in to catch, they should turn their glove over (fingers pointed down) only if they have to catch the ball below their waist. In all other cases, keep the fingers pointed up or

Whenever there is time, players should set up to catch the ball over the throwing shoulder (first photo). They should get behind the ball and catch it with two hands.

THE VALUE OF VERSATILITY

Players have a favorite or most comfortable position on the field. But it's to their advantage to learn how to play as many positions as possible.

Coaches at every level of the game view versatility as an asset. It makes a player more valuable to the team, and also increases that player's chance of playing every day. It's fun to play a position that is most comfortable, but the main objective is to be in the lineup. Whether that be playing shortstop, first base, or right field, the bottom line is to have a spot in the lineup and on the field.

slightly to the side. On balls above the waist, the glove acts like a windshield wiper, arcing back and forth depending on the ball's location.

Once players become efficient at employing the proper technique, they have to catch fly ball after fly ball after fly ball. This is the only way to develop judgment. Ground balls are easy to judge, but fly balls take time and practice. A great time for players to practice fly ball judgment is during team batting practice. It's the closest they'll get to the real thing in the game.

The Two-Week Preseason Training Plan for Fielders

Weeks One and Two: Monday Through Saturday

Monday	One-knee drill, game of 21, ground balls off the wall, pick-ups, drop steps, underhand/overhand fly balls
Tuesday	One-knee drill, long toss, ground balls A to Z, short hops, fly balls coming in
Wednesday	One-knee drill, game of 21, ground balls off the wall (backhand), pick-ups, drop steps, underhand/overhand fly balls
Thursday	One-knee drill, long toss, ground balls A to Z (to the left), short-hop drill, underhand/overhand fly balls, wide receiver drill
Friday	One-knee drill, game of 21, ground balls off the wall (glove side), quick exchange, wide receiver drill, fly ball mania
Saturday	One-knee drill, long toss, ground balls A to Z (to the right), charging ground balls, fly ball mania, fly balls off the bat

One-Knee Drill

We're stealing this drill from the pitchers, but it's an excellent exercise for developing proper throwing technique. Players place the knee of their post leg (right knee for a right-handed player) on the ground with their stride foot flat on the ground for balance. They hold their glove directly in front of their chest with their hand holding the ball in their glove. They rotate their shoulders and separate into the power position. Now they deliver the throw, making sure to extend the throwing arm down and across the stride leg and to pull the glove arm down and into their side. From a distance of approximately 20 feet, the players should throw 15 to 20 balls during this drill.

Game of 21

Playing catch allows players to get loose and build arm strength. Accuracy, however, is often the forgotten element of focus. The game of 21 improves a player's focus on throwing accuracy.

The one-knee drill is an excellent exercise for infielders and outfielders looking to polish their throwing form.

Pair two players and place them 30 to 40 feet apart. The targets are an imaginary rectangle formed at the top and bottom of the partner's shoulders and waist, and an imaginary rectangle around the partner's head. If a throw arrives within the chest rectangle, score a point. If it comes within the head boundaries, score two points. The first player to get to 21 points wins the game.

As players loosen up before practice and games, play a game of 21 to ensure they concentrate on hitting a target with each throw.

Long Toss

Long toss is a drill used for building arm strength. Players begin playing catch from approximately 40 feet and back up 5 feet every five throws. They continue moving back until they reach 70 feet. (Players with stronger arms may even be able to move back to 90 feet.) During the latter stages of this drill, players should not unleash high, arcing throws. They should keep the ball on a straight line. If they can no longer reach their partner in the air, they should do so on one bounce.

Ground Balls off the Wall

The only things necessary for this drill are a ball, glove, wall, and the desire to improve. Players throw the ball against the wall, shuffle their feet to get in front of it, and field the ground ball with an emphasis on proper technique. As the ball is fielded, they quickly shift their feet and align themselves for the next throw. Players

Long toss is one of the best methods of increasing arm strength. Outfielders especially should long toss every day.

To make long toss more interesting for players, use the soft-toss net as a target and create a friendly competition.

should vary the height of their throws to create different types of ground balls.

The players should field 25 ground balls per session. Soft hands and quick feet are marks of a good fielder. The better players get, the more they should challenge themselves to increase range.

A variation of this drill is to throw balls to the right and left and work on backhand plays and fielding the ball off the glove-side foot.

Pickups

A coach, parent, or player stands approximately 10 feet away with a baseball. The player is set in the fielder's position. The feeder rolls the ball a few feet to the player's right. The player shuffles to the right, fields the ball, and tosses it underhanded back to the feeder. The feeder then rolls the ball a few feet to the player's left, and the player shuffles to the left, fields the ball, and tosses it underhanded back to the feeder. This continues back and forth until the player has fielded 25 pickups.

Ground Balls A to Z

From approximately 60 to 90 feet, a coach or parent hits a ground ball to the fielder. If the player fields the ball cleanly (without bobbling it), the player calls out the last name of a major-league player that starts with the letter *A*. If the next ball is fielded cleanly, the player calls out the last name of a player that starts with the letter *B*. This continues until the fielder gets all the way through the alphabet. It's a fun way of fielding 25 ground balls without error. (I know, there are 26 letters in the alphabet, but no player in major league history has had a last name that started with the letter *X*.)

Short-Hop Drill

Two players (or a player and an adult) stand approximately 10 feet apart. Each has feet spread wide, knees bent deep, rear end low to the ground, and glove extended in the ready position. They make

Infielders enjoy making a game out of the short-hop drill. First one to get three balls past his or her partner wins.

short-hop throws back and forth to each other. (A short hop is when the ball hits the ground just in front of the player.) Players should not move their feet in this drill, but rather isolate their glove hand and work on picking balls. Continue throwing back and forth until each player has fielded 20 short hops.

Quick Exchange

Two players stand 15 feet apart in an athletic position (knees bent, feet slightly farther than shoulder-width apart). The object is to throw the ball back and forth, concentrating on transferring the ball from glove to hand as quickly as possible. There are three points of focus to stress:

1. Reach for the ball. The sooner you receive the ball, the faster you can get it into throwing position.
2. Catch the ball in the palm of your glove. This makes it easy to grab the ball with your throwing hand. Catching it in the web forces you to dig it out of the glove.
3. Catch the ball with two hands. Having your throwing hand positioned next to the glove reduces the transfer time.

Instruct players to try to develop a rhythm where they're c:
ing the ball, transferring it from glove to hand, and throwing it
continuous motion. Balls should not be thrown hard, but rather
crisply and accurately. Use a stopwatch to see how long it takes to
throw the ball back and forth 15 times. Each practice, players
should try to beat their best time.

Underhand/Overhand Fly Balls

This drill is used to teach proper technique and eliminate the element of fear. Standing 30 feet away, toss balls underhanded approximately 15 to 20 feet in the air. The player should focus on moving
to the point of the ball's descent, getting in the proper position, and
catching the ball with two hands. The player's head (and eyes)
remain still, locked on the ball.

Gradually move back and toss balls overhand. Increase the height
of the throws as the player's comfort and confidence builds.

Drop Steps

Baseballs are not necessary for this drill. With the outfielder poised
in the ready position, call out, "Drop step right!" The player takes
his right foot and swings it back to the right. This opens the hips
so he can run to a ball that is hit overhead to the right. The player
runs three or four strides after taking the drop step. Continue with
at least five drop steps to the right and five to the left, varying what
is called each time.

Fly Balls Coming In

Stand approximately 60 to 80 feet from the outfielder. Call out,
"Break!" The outfielder runs directly toward you at full speed. Toss
the ball (at varying heights) so the player must catch the ball below
the waist. The outfielder's glove should be turned over so the fingers of the glove are pointed down. Continue for 10 to 15 tosses.
This is a difficult play for outfielders, but an enjoyable drill.

74

From the set position, the outfielder drops his right leg back to open his hips. He then runs back to the point of the ball's descent and reaches up to make the running catch.

Wide Receiver Drill

The coach or parent plays quarter-back and the outfielder plays wide receiver. On the call of "Hike!" the player sprints out a designated pattern. The tosser lofts the ball in the air so the outfielder catches the ball on the run.

Vary the pass patterns, running straight, diagonal, cuts, and so on. Outfielders should be reminded to run on their toes, not on their heels. Running on the toes allows the head to remain as still as possible, keeping the eyes locked on the baseball.

Fly Ball Mania

This drill is a lot of fun for out-fielders and works on drop steps, three types of fly balls, and throwing. The outfielder begins facing you, approximately 3 feet away. On the call "Break!" the out-fielder takes a drop step to the right. Allow the player to run 30 feet and toss the ball over his right shoulder. Immediately after catching the ball, the outfielder must plant his feet, align his body with the tosser, and make a strong return throw. After throwing the

On running catches coming in, the outfielder turns his glove palm-up to make the play.

75

Fly ball mania is a fun drill that combines outfield play and conditioning.

ball, he must immediately break to the left, running a straight line across. The tosser catches the return throw and delivers a line-drive throw to the outfielder's left that reaches him on the run. The outfielder catches the ball, plants, delivers a strong return throw, and runs directly at the tosser. The tosser catches the return throw and delivers a short fly ball that the outfielder has to catch below the waist on his way in.

Outfielders love this drill, and it works on a variety of skills. After starting the outfielders to their right a few times, start them to the left and reverse the direction of throws.

Fly Balls Off the Bat

With the outfielder positioned approximately 100 feet away, hit fly balls off the bat. Try to simulate the height of hits in a Little League game, not a major-league game. Even if the player has trouble catching balls, use this drill to develop judgment. Hit at least 15 to 20 balls each practice.

A quick tip, if it's not obvious to you already: Once the proper technique for hitting, pitching, and fielding are in place, it's all about repetition. Players have to practice religiously so they can execute without thought in games. The different drills and games are created in part to maintain their attention. To get better at fielding ground balls, players have to field more ground balls. To hit more consistently, they have to take more swings off the tee and in batting practice. Getting better is not rocket science. It's about practice.

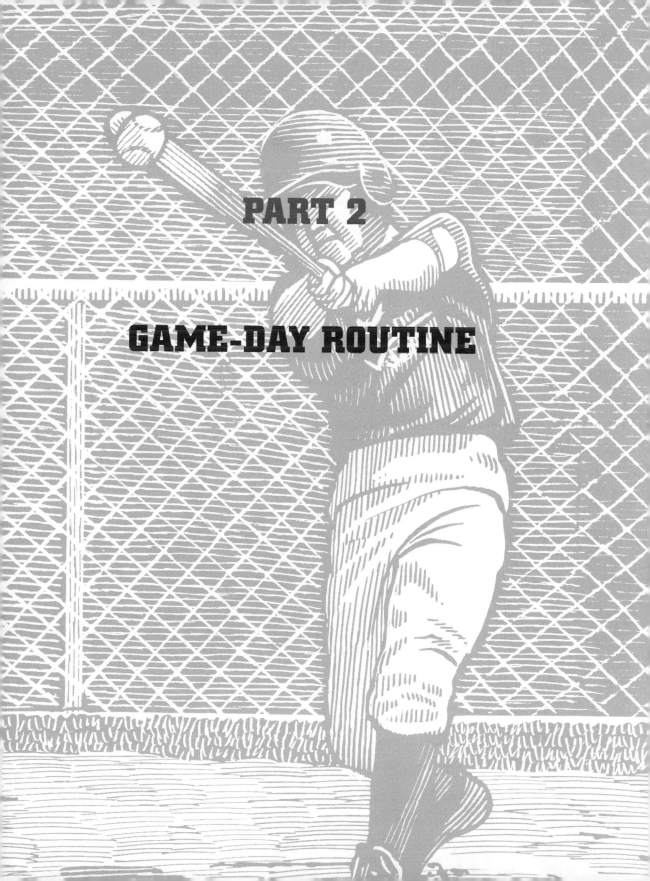

PART 2

GAME-DAY ROUTINE

5

PREGAME PREPARATION AND STRETCHES

Nothing is more exciting for kids than game day. All the practice and instruction is helpful and enjoyable, but it pales in comparison to suiting up in uniform and crossing over the white lines to play the game. There is still some coaching that takes place before and during the game, but game day is primarily a time for execution.

The ride over to the field offers an opportunity to give players a great start to their day. For a short time, refresh their memory regarding some of the skills they've been working on in practice. Perhaps they have been dropping their hands before swinging the bat and could benefit from a quick reminder to avoid old habits. Don't drill them on it, just a subtle reminder. Also, let them know if they play aggressively, play smart, and play with passion, then they can expect good things to happen. Everything should be geared toward positive thought. When kids are in a positive mind-set, they play more relaxed and with greater self-assurance. And in that state of mind, improved play will follow.

The very last thing young players need before a game is the pressure of high expectations. If the players are competitive by nature, the desire to do well will come from within. If they are not the competitive type, that is okay, too. It's simply not a personality trait, at least not in this particular environment. External pressures to perform are unnecessary and will prove to be counterproductive, and that is not isolated to the baseball field. Put your relationship with your children first.

Baseball is a game. One more time: it's a *game*. As former major-league pitcher and manager Bob Lemon once said, "Baseball is a kid's game that grown-ups only tend to mess up." Many valuable lessons are learned through participating in athletics, several that can't be learned in the classroom at school. But it's extremely important to maintain perspective and keep in mind that in the end, it's just a game.

The best way parents can assist their players is to show support and remain positive before, during, and after the game.

Pregame stretching is extremely important and should be done as a team.

Pregame Stretching

The game of baseball is a series of short, explosive movements. Swinging a bat, throwing a baseball, racing to the left to spear a hard-hit ground ball—these all require quickness and power. Stretching the entire body effectively not only allows players to perform these movements with greater capability, but it also reduces the risk of injury.

Please take the time to adequately stretch players. It's up to the adults to mandate stretching because Little League players will not do it on their own. It's boring to them and they don't see any immediate reward. Be very strict on this topic because you're not just stretching kids out for their game, you're also developing their habits for the future.

As you've read in the earlier parts of this book, baseball players use their entire body to properly execute the mechanics of hitting, throwing, and fielding the baseball. With this in mind, it's im-

Ankle
stretch

perative that the entire body is attended to during pregame stretching.

To adequately teach these stretches, try them yourself and learn exactly where players should feel their muscles stretch.

Ankle Stretch

Lift your foot off the ground and balance on one leg. Point your toe toward the ground and make circles with your foot to loosen the ankle joint. Make 10 circles and then switch feet. After completing two sets of 10, make counterclockwise circles with your feet 10 times.

Calf and Achilles Tendon Stretch

Lean against a fence, dugout, or teammate with your hands pressed firmly against the object you're leaning on. Move one leg 8 to 10 inches backward, keeping both feet flat on the ground. Bend the front knee forward and allow the heel of the rear foot to rise off the ground. Keep the toe of your rear foot on the ground. Hold the stretch for 10 seconds and then switch legs. Continue until you complete three sets of stretches for each leg.

Upper Hamstring Stretch

Lie flat on your back. Bend your left leg at the knee and raise it toward your midsection. Grab the shin of your left leg with both hands and pull into your midsection. Pull your knee toward your chin as far as possible. Your right leg and back should remain flat on the ground. Hold the stretch for 10 seconds and then

Upper hamstring stretch

switch legs. Complete three sets for each leg.

Lower Hamstring Stretch

Standing erect with your feet close together, cross your right foot over your left foot and bend at the waist. Grab your ankles or feet (whatever your flexibility allows) with both hands. Hold the stretch for 10 seconds and switch. Try to increase your stretch with each set.

Lower hamstring stretch

Quadriceps
stretch

Quadriceps Stretch

Standing erect, bend your right leg at the knee so your right foot rises behind you. Reach down with your right hand and grab the instep of your right foot. Pull your foot up to your buttocks, while maintaining your balance on your left leg. Pull until you feel a stretch in your quadriceps muscle. Hold the stretch for 10 seconds and then relax and switch legs.

Groin Stretch

Sit on the ground with your legs crossed. Move your feet so the soles are pressed against each other. Grab the tops of your feet with

84

Groin stretch

both hands and pull them up. Your elbows should touch the insides of your knees and press down. Hold for 10 seconds, relax, and then repeat.

Torso Stretch

Sit on the ground with your legs stretched outward in front of you. Bend your right leg at the knee, slide your right foot inward toward your buttocks, and grab your right knee with both hands. Next, lift your right foot over your left leg and place it on the outside of your left knee. Put your right hand on the ground by your right side (for balance) and place your left hand on the outside of your right knee. Pull the knee to the left to feel a stretch in the right portion of your torso. Hold for 10 seconds and switch sides.

Torso stretch

Lower back stretch

Lower Back

Lie flat on your stomach on the ground. Use both hands to push your upper body up off the ground, but keep your entire lower body (from the waist down) pressed against the ground. Hold this position for 10 seconds and then rest. Repeat this four or five times to stretch the lower back.

Upper back stretch

Upper Back

Holding your hands out in front of you, lock them together with your fingers. Raise your hands above your head and stretch your arms up toward the sky. Turn your hands over so your palms face the sky. Hold your arms up in this extend position for 15 seconds. Rest and repeat four to five times.

Forearms

Extend your right arm out in front of you and turn your hand over so your palm faces the sky. Grab the right-hand fingers with your left hand and pull them down. Keep the right arm extended as you do this. Hold the stretch for 10 seconds and then switch arms. Next, allow the palm to face down and pull up on the fingers. Hold this stretch for 10 seconds and then switch. Repeat each stretch three times.

Forearm stretch

Triceps stretch

Triceps

Lift your right arm directly over your right shoulder. Reach over your head with your left hand, grab your right elbow, and pull it back. Pull it back as far as it can go without experiencing pain. Hold the stretch for 10 seconds and switch arms. Stretch each arm for three sets.

Shoulder Stretch

Lay your right arm across your chest. Grab your right elbow with your left hand and pull your right arm up and to the left. Hold the stretch for 10 seconds and then relax. Repeat the same exercise, this time pulling your left arm across your body. Stretch each arm for three sets.

Shoulder stretch

89

Running Form

One of the most underappreciated aspects of the game is running. Hitting, pitching, and fielding receive the lion's share of the attention, but what about running? How do players get a run tacked up on the scoreboard? They do so by running from home to first to second to third and then crossing back over home plate. Greater emphasis should be placed on baserunning, and the first step in improving players' baserunning skills is to enhance their running form.

Below is a list of the most common mistakes made by young runners.

- *Tension.* To maximize speed and quickness, the body must remain relaxed. Much like swinging a baseball bat or throwing a pitch, tension forces the muscles to contract, which slows everything down. Fast runners keep their body loose as they sprint.

- *Leaning back.* In an effort to run as fast as possible, players often tilt their upper body back. When moving forward, you want your entire body working together. If your legs are racing forward and the upper half of the body is leaning back, it hinders momentum. Runners should lean forward slightly with the upper body.

- *Failure to pump arms.* It's true that the legs are the major source of energy when sprinting, but the arms (and upper body) can help generate additional speed. World-class track runners are a perfect example of athletes who use their upper body as well as their lower body when running. As the right knee rises, the left arm pumps upward.

- *Heel stepping.* This major flaw can be seen in runners of all ages. Players commonly land on their heel as their foot hits the ground. The front portion of the foot then has to contact the ground before springing back up off the ball of the foot. It's only a split second, but if a runner is taking an additional fraction of a second with every stride, it adds up. The spring in a sprinter's step comes from the ball of the foot. If the foot lands on the ball of the foot (or closer to the front of the foot), the runner can quickly spring into the next step. It's a minor point, but a major factor in running speed.

After players are stretched out, a few running form and agility drills can go a long way in improving individual and team speed.

Arm Pumps

With their feet stationary, players pump their arms up and down. They should keep their hands relaxed, bend at the elbows, and thrust their arms up and down, starting near their hip and rising up toward the side of their head. Arm pumps should be up and down, not side to side. They should alternate—right, left, right, left—as fast as possible.

Running in Place

Players practice landing on the balls of their feet by running in place. Each time a foot lands, they should spring upward off the ball of the foot. As they get comfortable, they should pump their arms in unison. As the left knee rises, the right arm pumps upward.

Practice pumping the arms to incorporate the upper body into running form.

Once this has been mastered, the players should lean forward at the waist and slowly begin to run forward. This is a form drill, not a race. Players should maintain proper form—balls of the feet, arms pumping—as they run.

91

Striders

Using the same technique applied in the initial running-form drills, players extend their stride as far as possible with each step. Again, this is not a race. By stretching out their stride even marginally, players are eating up more ground and reducing the distance from point A to point B when running. Instruct players to spring off the ball of the foot and

Run in place while keeping focus on pumping the arms.

The high-knees drill trains runners to become more explosive with each step.

reach out with the leg as they stride.

High Knees

Players start by running in place, exaggerating how high their knees elevate with each repetition. They should pump their knees as their arms pump, and spring off the balls of their feet. After about 15 seconds of running in place, they should lean forward slightly and slowly run forward, keeping the knees pumping high and gradually advancing into a full sprint.

Agility Drills

Agility drills help develop speed, quickness, and obviously, agility. Moving back to catch a fly ball, racing forward to field a bunt, and changing direction on the base path all require agility. If you have time before games, agility drills are an excellent method of getting players ready for game action. If you're pressed for time before a game, make sure to include agility drills before or after practice.

Lateral Line Jumps

Using the right-field foul line, players stand on the foul-territory side of the line facing home plate. They place both feet together and position them so they're standing right next to the line. (Their feet are now parallel to the foul line.) Keeping both feet together, they jump up and over the foul line, landing in fair territory. Without hesitation, they then jump back over to the foul-territory side, and continue jumping back and forth for 30 seconds. They should do their best to maintain balance. Have the players count how many jumps they perform in 30 seconds and work to increase that number each time out. (If no foul lines are available, you can have players jump over a hat or a glove.)

Forward/Backward Line Jumps

Players turn their feet so they are perpendicular to the foul line and the players are facing the outfield. Keeping their feet together, they leap forward over the foul line into fair territory. Upon landing, they immediately jump backward over the line into foul territory. They continue jumping forward and backward for 30 seconds. Have the players count how many jumps they perform in 30 seconds and work to increase that number each time out.

Lateral and forward/backward line jumps improve agility and develop explosiveness.

UTILIZING YOUR COACHING STAFF

The best way to run a baseball team is to delegate some responsibility to the assistant coaches. There are simply too many facets of the game for one person to control efficiently.

Here are some departments where you can put an assistant coach in charge: outfielders, infielders, pitchers, stretching, pregame infield/outfield practice, throwing batting practice, and keeping the scorebook.

Obviously, the head coach or manager will assume several of these responsibilities, but entrusting some of these roles to assistants can allow the person in charge to focus on the overall team and game management.

Following Orders

Players stand in the outfield grass or anywhere that gives them plenty of space. They face a coach or teammate and respond by moving in the direction of his or her command. The caller's job is to call out and point up, back, right, or left. If the caller yells, "back," players backpedal until they're given the next command. If the caller points to the players' left and yells, "left," they shuffle to the left until they hear the next command. Players should continue following orders for 45 seconds before resting.

Loosening the Throwing Arm

Stretching and running-form drills get the body limber, but the throwing arm requires special attention before games. Throwing is an unnatural motion, and if a player starts uncorking throws without warming up, it could lead to soreness or injury.

First, take the team into the outfield. Pair up players, having one stand on the outfield foul line facing his or her teammate, who is standing in the outfield grass. Have infielders play catch with infielders, outfielders with outfielders, and catchers with catchers. Throwing routines differ slightly depending on position, so players should partner up with teammates who play similar positions. Players should position themselves approximately 20 feet apart to start and focus on proper throwing form.

Remind players that the purpose of pregame throwing is to get their arms loose and practice throwing form and accuracy. It's not a contest to see who can throw the hardest or farthest. If there are players who have a little more difficulty with catching and throwing, have a coach catch with them so the player can benefit from personal instruction.

Playing catch before the game or practice is a time to get the arms loose and work on throwing form.

After 8 to 10 throws, the line of players in the outfield takes three steps back. Players should continue to take two to three steps backward every five throws. Once players get to a point where their arms are loose, infielders, outfielders, and catchers should break into specific exercises for the final part of pregame throwing.

Infielders should shorten the distance of their throws and work on quick exchange. (The quick-exchange drill is described in Chapter 4.) Outfielders should continue to stretch their throws and long toss (also covered in Chapter 4). Catchers should stand 75 to 90 feet apart and practice throws to second base. From the catcher's stance, they should pop out of their squat and fire a throw to their teammate.

Allow approximately 15 minutes for pregame throwing. It should only take 10 minutes, but it's better to have extra time to loosen up than too little. Cold days require additional time to get loose, while warm days entail a bit less.

6

GETTING PLAYERS READY FOR THE FIRST PITCH

O nce the players are stretched out and their arms are loose, it's time to start preparing them for the start of the game. Most of this is accomplished through physical exercises, but some time should be spent reviewing practice notes and making sure players are in a positive frame of mind. Infield/outfield practice, swinging bats, warming up the pitcher, and pregame talks are part of the customary routine that gets players ready before the first pitch is thrown.

Before infield/outfield practice is taken, it's the responsibility of the coach to walk the field to check for conditions. Any information from the field check must be communicated to the players. This proves helpful for player performance and safety.

Any information that is to be imparted to the players should be done before infield/outfield practice. If field conditions are going to influence defensive positioning or the manner in which balls are played, players should employ their adjustments during pregame practice.

Send players out to their positions and make sure they hustle. Players should run from the dugout all the way out to their posi-

FIELD CHECK CHECKLIST

- Condition of the infield grass: long, short, dry, wet
- Condition of the infield dirt: hard, soft, wet, uneven
- Condition of the outfield grass: long, short, wet, potholes, slant
- Condition of the pitching mound: high, low, deep holes
- Distance between home plate and backstop
- Position of the sun (and where it will be throughout the game)
- Warning track
- Unique structures that can influence infield or outfield play
- Space between fence and ground

tion. It looks good, but it also acts as a signal to players that game time is nearing and it's time to focus. The coach hitting infield/outfield practice should be equipped with a fungo bat and five or six baseballs. If balls are missed or overthrown, you want to continue to keep a rhythm.

All players take the field during infield/outfield practice, not just starters. Nonstarters will get into the game eventually and should be given the opportunity to field balls from their position before game time. In addition, it's good for team morale and makes all the players feel like they're contributing prior to the game. If there are two shortstops on the team, have both of them at shortstop for pregame infield/outfield. Do try to avoid an overload of players at one position, however, as it will slow down tempo.

Pregame Outfield Practice

Outfielders are hit to first. Left fielders throw to second base, and center and right fielders throw to third base. Hit two ground balls to the left fielder; one directly at the fielder and one to his or her right. Emphasize accurate throws to the base. Second basemen should take throws at second base from the left fielder. The first baseman should back up the throw.

Hit two ground balls to the center fielder. Hit the first directly at the player and the second to the player's left or right. Emphasize accurate throws to the base. The shortstop acts as the cutoff man on the throw and should be aligned directly between third base and the position the center fielder gloves the ball. It's the responsibility of the third baseman to line up the shortstop for the cutoff. A pitcher should run off the mound and back up third base.

Hit two ground balls to the right fielder. Hit the first directly at the player and the second to the player's right. Emphasize accurate throws to the base. The shortstop acts as the cutoff man and (again) is lined up by the third baseman. The second baseman covers second base and a pitcher should run off the mound and back up third base.

A crisp infield/outfield puts the team in a confident state of mind before game time.

Hitting fly balls to the outfield during pregame is crucial. It allows outfielders to see how the ball is carrying, and also gets them familiar with the background that balls will be hit from during the game.

The second round of balls hit to the outfield are thrown home. Hit a ground ball to the left fielder followed by a high fly ball. On throws home from left field, the third baseman acts as the cutoff man, the shortstop covers third base, and the second baseman covers second base. The catcher aligns the third baseman between home plate and the origin of the throw. The pitcher should back up home plate.

On balls thrown home from center and right field, the first baseman is the cutoff man. The catcher aligns the first baseman with the throw while the third baseman covers third, the shortstop covers second, and the pitcher backs up home plate. First base is left open.

After you've completed the second round of hitting balls to the outfield, have an assistant coach trot out to the foul line with a fungo bat and baseballs. All outfielders should move toward center field and shag fly balls. Have the assistant hit balls to the outfielders while you continue with pregame infield practice. (If your team's dugout is on the third-base side, hit balls from the third-base foul line and vice versa.)

Pregame Infield Practice

A crisp infield practice can set the tone for the game. Promote high standards during this phase of pregame so players come off the field feeling good about the game they are about to enter.

The first round of ground balls are hit directly to the player and thrown to first base. Hit a routine ground ball to the third baseman, shortstop, second baseman, and first baseman, and then roll a bunt out for the catcher to field and throw to first. Hit balls to the infielders' left during the second round of ground balls. Again, the play is to first base.

Call out "Let's get two!" for the next two rounds of ground balls. The second baseman covers the base on ground balls hit to third base and shortstop, receives the throw, and then fires to first base to complete the double play. The shortstop covers second base on ground balls hit to the second baseman, first baseman, and catcher. Hit the first round of double-play balls directly at the position player and the second round of double-play balls to the players' left or right. (Force them to react.)

101

Routine ground balls during infield practice allow players to read how quick the infield plays. This helps dictate how deep to play and how aggressively to move forward on ground balls during the game.

For the final round, call out, "One and in!" Have each fielder back up a few steps and play deep. Hit a ground ball to the players' right to force a long throw to first base. After they make the throw to first, the fielders should move forward to play a second ground ball. This ball should be fielded and fired home for a tag play at the plate. Repeat this for each fielder at third base, shortstop, second base, and first base. After the first baseman has completed the throw to the plate (and if you're really good), hit a foul pop-up to the catcher to complete infield/outfield practice. Hitting a high pop to the catcher isn't as hard as it seems. Toss the ball up high and slice under the backside of the ball with a severe uppercut. The best way to learn is through trial and error.

The momentum of a game can shift to your favor by turning a defensive double play.

COACHING FROM THE THIRD-BASE BOX

The best piece of advice to a coach who constantly shouts instruction to hitters from the third-base box is to *keep quiet*! As a coach, it's understandable that you want to help the hitter at the plate. But by calling out two, three, or four different hitting tips as a kid stands in the box, you're disrupting the hitter's concentration. In addition, you may make the hitter nervous or angry. Emotions must be very calm to swing the bat effectively.

Let the hitter learn through trial and error. If there is something the player is doing that must be addressed, do it after the game or at practice. The game is a time for execution, not persecution. Keep the chatter to a bare minimum.

103

Warming Up the Bats

With the majority of Little League games being played on weeknights, there isn't enough time to have batting practice before games. Parents are usually in a hurry just to get their children to the field on time. With time being such a critical factor, there are some quick exercises that enable hitters to ready themselves for competition.

Take the team into the outfield and spread them out so they have enough space to swing the bat. Have the players get into their batting stance and take a few slow-motion swings (discussed in Chapter 2) to stress sound fundamentals. After they've completed a few swings, have them shift their attention to you (or another coach) facing them from a distance.

For the next five minutes, the team will work on visualization swings. The coach simulates a pitcher's windup, swings his or her arm up to deliver an imaginary pitch, and at just about the point of release, calls out a pitch and location. For example, "fastball down the middle," or, "fastball, low on the outside corner," or, "fastball, up on the inside corner." Hitters should visualize the pitch coming in and execute a game-speed swing based on the pitch location. After imaginary contact is made, they are to visualize the end result, which is always positive. For a fastball down the middle, they should imagine a line drive back through the middle. For a fastball down and away, they should visualize a line drive to the opposite field, and so forth.

This exercise not only warms up the body, but it kick-starts the mind, which controls what the body does. Visualization drills are extremely beneficial. Use this to prepare your batters physically, mentally, and emotionally.

Portable soft-toss nets are the perfect solution when playing at a field that doesn't permit hitting balls into a fence.

Some teams are equipped with a portable soft-toss net. This can also be used for soft-toss drills. Make sure you practice common sense to avoid any dangers or accidents. Assume a ball will be hit over the net, so be careful of the direction players are hitting.

Warming Up the Pitcher

Warming up the starting pitcher should involve more than the pitcher simply running down to the bullpen and throwing a dozen

HOW TO RUN BATTING PRACTICE

Say, for example, that you have 12 players on your team. Form three hitting groups with 4 players in each group. Have group one come in to hit while groups two and three remain in the field to catch ground balls and fly balls.

The first batter in group one gets six swings. On the sixth swing, the batter runs to first base on the hit and becomes a base runner while the other hitters in the group take their swings. Each hitter runs out his or her last hit (sixth swing). This allows players to practice baserunning during batting practice.

Each hitter takes six swings in the first round. The second round they take five swings, and finally a third round of three swings. After the third round, group two comes in to hit and group one takes the field.

This is the most proficient way to take batting practice. Your team is practicing hitting, fielding, and baserunning at the same time. Keep the number of swings per round to a minimum. Too many swings tire young hitters and can create bad habits. It also bores other players if one player is hitting for too long.

pitches. According to pitching expert and author Randy Voorhees, it should include running, stretching, throwing, and finally, warm-up pitches. Develop a consistent routine for pitchers so they know exactly what they need to accomplish before each start.

Running

Running should be in the form of a brief jog, perhaps two minutes in duration. Running warms up the muscles and gets the blood flowing. Have the pitcher jog from foul pole to foul pole twice to be ready for the next stage of the warm-up.

Stretching

The pitcher should have stretched with the rest of the team, but it's better to be safe than sorry. Run through stretches discussed in Chapter 5, working from the ground up. Once properly stretched, the pitcher can move on to the throwing stage of the warm-up.

Throwing

The pitcher should begin the throwing phase by tossing lightly to the catcher—on flat ground—at a distance of 35 to 40 feet. After 10 throws, have the pitcher move back to 45 feet (ten throws), then to 50 feet (ten throws), then to 60 feet (five throws). After each move back, the pitcher should add more velocity to the throws, so the last few are close to full speed.

Warm-Up Pitches

Warm-up pitches are thrown off the mound, provided there is one in the bullpen. If there is not a pitching mound, have the pitcher throw in the direction he or she will be throwing in the game. (Wind can often be a factor when pitching, so you want to simulate game conditions as best as you can.) Here are some general guidelines for warm-up pitches that your pitchers should follow:

- Throw a high percentage of fastballs (at least 75 percent).
- Begin and end with a fastball.
- Throw all but the last few pitches at less than maximum exertion.
- Always throw to a very precise location.
- Throw no more than 35 to 40 pitches.
- Pause for a few seconds between pitches.

Allow enough time for warm-ups in the bullpen so that your pitcher has at least two or three minutes before the game starts. This gives the pitcher a little time to rest and also review the game plan before heading out to the mound. Remember, the pitcher is given up to eight pitches to throw from the mound before facing the first batter.

A coach should always be with the pitcher warming up in the bullpen. Coaches can give instruction, supportive advice, and make sure the pitcher stays disciplined during warm-ups.

POSITIVE TALK FROM DUGOUT TO THE PITCHER'S MOUND

If you have ever been to a Little League baseball game, it's almost guaranteed you have heard this call (or at least some variation) from the dugout, "You've got to throw strikes."

Now, it's true that a 10-year-old kid doesn't know everything, but do you think he doesn't know that? Would anyone think for one second a pitcher isn't trying to throw strikes?

The pitching mound can be a very lonely place to be during a game. Some kids relish the spotlight, while others do not. Having a good arm does not necessarily mean a player likes to pitch or enjoys the pressure. Throwing strikes can be difficult, especially in a tight situation.

The best thing a coach can do is to shout out encouragement. This enables the pitcher to relax and impresses upon the player that this is not a life-or-death situation. If the player is still having trouble and is visibly upset, relieve him or her from the situation. Put another pitcher in the game, and congratulate the player for trying his or her best.

108

Pregame Talk

One of the toughest aspects of coaching (in any sport) is that you can't control what the players do out on the field. Once the pitcher toes the rubber in baseball, the game is (for the most part) out of the hands of parents and coaches. Throwing strikes, hitting breaking balls, or catching pop flies rests squarely on the shoulders of the kids on the field. And that's the way it should be. We (adults) have

Pregame discussions should be informative, but also kept light. Baseball players perform best when they are loose and relaxed.

109

had our time, and it's now the kids' turn to have their fun between the white lines.

Coaches can help players *prepare* for competition, and the final phase of preparation is pregame discussions. Make the most out of the few minutes spent in the dugout. Review one or two situational plays on defense, read the starting and reserve lineups, and instill positive thoughts in the team's minds before the umpire calls out, "Play ball!"

Review of Game Situations

A few things that you might go over before the game starts are some simple reminders on defense. For example, discuss where each position player should go if the batter squares to bunt with a runner on second base. Players should orally respond to where they should go, whether it be an infielder covering a base or an outfielder backing up a throw.

A rundown play is often a sanctuary for defensive blunders in Little League games. Remind players that they should minimize the number of throws in a rundown situation and force the base runner to commit to running to one base or the other. (Rundown plays and bunt coverage are discussed in detail in Chapter 8.) Outfield cutoffs, steals, and force plays are also situational plays on defense that are worth reviewing in a pregame talk and are discussed in detail in Chapter 8.

Reading the Lineup

Only nine players can be in the lineup at once. Those are the rules of Little League baseball. Teams usually consist of a roster of 12 to 15 players, which obviously means several players will not be in the starting lineup. This is a reality that players must learn and understand and many will, but there are several ways to go about trying to cushion the blow in the eyes and ears of those who may get upset.

One method is to have a set plan how players will be substituted and to include that plan in the pregame talk. With lineup in hand, say, "Okay, this is how we're going to start." Read off the starting lineup, and then follow it with the inning and position each substitute player will enter the game. First, they will feel included, and second, they'll know exactly when they're going in the game so they can adequately prepare themselves. Believe me, players would much rather know when they're going in the game rather than flattering them with the element of surprise.

Another method is to have your starting lineup rotate. If you have 12 players, for example, formulate four groups of 3 players. Every fourth game, a group of 3 players starts on the bench. Within that group, have an infielder, outfielder, and a pitcher or catcher.

Players may not be able to play the exact same position each time out, but the great thing about that is they learn to play various positions and become more versatile. Versatility has great benefits in later years.

There will always be a case (or cases) where parents or players are unhappy. Welcome to coaching. The best thing to do is to listen to the issue at hand and then calmly explain your reasoning as doing what is best for the team and the players as a whole. Do not react with emotion and don't take criticisms personally. It will only lead to bigger problems.

Positive Talk

After reading the lineup, fill the players' heads with positive talk. Stay away from negative words like "no," "don't," "never," and so on. You want your team to play to win, not to play to not lose. There is a big difference. Playing to not make mistakes fosters a timid, hesitant mind-set, which leads to flawed play.

Call for players to compete aggressively, to go out and make great plays, to drive the ball with authority. Above all, tell players to go out and have fun. Enjoy the game. Baseball is a game and it should be nothing other than a great experience for kids.

PART 3

IN-SEASON MAINTENANCE

7

KEEPING PLAYERS SHARP AND CORRECTING MISTAKES

Part 3 is broken into two parts of in-season maintenance. This chapter explores how to maintain and sharpen individual skills during the season. Strengths and weaknesses on offense and defense will surface as the season progresses. The object is to embellish strengths and to improve or eliminate weaknesses. Chapter 8 discusses situational plays that emerge during games that must be addressed in practice. Rundowns, bunt coverage, first-and-third defenses, and cutoff plays are significant to recording outs and keeping runs off the scoreboard.

Player Maintenance

Baseball has become a year-round sport. Games begin in the early spring, continue throughout the summer, and now roll right into fall leagues. Even teams in the northeastern part of the United States are playing baseball nine or ten months out of the year. Players are now out-of-season for a very short period of time and in-season for the majority of the time.

With kids having busy schedules, practices are few and far between. This puts even more importance on organizing a productive workout when there is an opportunity to practice. But it also places responsibility on players to polish their skills individually. There is not enough time in a practice for each player to get his or her individual work in, so it has to be done on the players' own time. This can't be stressed enough. The very best players all do additional work on their own when no one is watching.

The physical benefits from skill work during the season are obvious. Repetitious training maintains muscle memory and allows players to execute instinctively. It also keeps the baseball muscles strong, so that bat speed and arm speed, quickness, and agility are performed at their optimum levels. Any rough edges that are evident during the season can be smoothed out as overall player development continues to progress.

116

There are psychological benefits as well. Hard work builds confidence, but it can also rebuild a bruised ego if a player is struggling during the season. There are several avenues players can travel to reverse their fortunes on the playing field, and extra ground balls, batting practice, and/or bullpen sessions are right to follow.

Hitting is fun, but it's the most difficult aspect of the game in which to maintain consistency.

Hitters

Throughout an entire season, there will be times when players are hitting everything that is thrown at them and times when their bat can't find its way to the ball. Hitters are often judged by their batting average, and it's important to understand that term. It's a batting *average*. Let's say, for example, a player is batting .400. At some points in the season, that player may have been a .600 hitter, and at other times a .200 hitter. But on *average*, this player is a .400 hitter.

One trait good hitters have is that they minimize the amount of time they are struggling and extend the time they're streaking. That's when batting averages soar. Also, from an emotional standpoint, it's essential that hitters never get too high or too low. Don't allow players to become so confident that they stop working to improve or lose respect for their opponent (the pitcher). Sooner rather than later, their performance will begin to slide. And don't let them get down on themselves. This will result in unnecessary stress or tension, or even worse, diminished confidence.

Cutting the Slump Short

The first step to fixing anything is to isolate the root of the problem. Not everyone is an expert on hitting, so at times it can be difficult to determine why a player is struggling at the plate. It may be caused by the mechanics of the swing, possibly the hitter's approach at the plate, or it may very well be mental. Quite often with Little League hitters, what they are thinking has a major effect on what their swing is doing. Ask the hitter some questions first to gather information before tinkering with the player's stance or swing.

Mental Mistakes

Are you thinking about pulling every pitch? This is a very common thought among young players because that is where they hit the ball hardest—when they pull it. Unfortunately, if they think "pull," their stride foot, front shoulder, swing, and head will pull off of the ball toward the pull side of the field. *Common results:*

Slumps are often due to poor swing mechanics, but it may be the hitter's preswing thoughts that are causing those flawed swings.

Strong hits on inside strikes, but weak hits on pitches thrown to the outside part of the plate; also the all-too-familiar look of the hitter's rear end sticking out on the pitches outside. As the hitter's body begins to pull off the ball, the eyes recognize the pitch is outside. The upper body fights the lower body to stay over home plate and the rear end sticks out.

Are you trying to hit the ball over the outfielder's head every time up? By trying to swing too hard, the hitter's rear shoulder often dips and he or she pulls up and off the ball. Tension will also become a factor and slow the swing down. *Common results:* Chopped ground balls to the pull side, pop-ups, lazy fly balls to the opposite field, and swings and misses.

Are you hoping to just put the bat on the ball? Hitters often feel for the pitch just so they can put it in play. They're actually afraid to swing and miss, which is something they should never fear. Their body then drifts toward the pitch and the bat drags to the ball. They attempt to place the bat on the ball, instead of firing the barrel with authority with the thought of driving the ball. The swing will appear as if the hitter pulls the bat to the ball and then flips the barrel at the pitch. *Common results:* Weakly hit balls to the opposite-field side, swings and misses on inside strikes, and a lot of called strikes.

Are you assuming the pitch is going to be a ball and then swinging if you see it's a strike? Hitters should anticipate strikes on every pitch. They should stride as the pitch is delivered and believe it's going to be a strike. That gets them in a good hitting position early enough to get the barrel out front once the pitch arrives. If it's a ball, there's time to hold up on the swing. If hitters think "ball" and all of a sudden it's a strike, they play catch-up with their swing as if they're rushing. *Common results:* Poor timing on pitches, hitting balls almost out of the catcher's glove to the opposite field, never seeming to get the barrel out to pull pitches.

Are you afraid the ball might hit you? This is devastating to hitters and extremely common among Little League–aged players. The unfortunate truth is, hitters who are afraid of the ball are never going to be able to hit. The first of two exercises that can fight that fear is for the hitter to see pitch after pitch after pitch. It establishes a greater degree of comfort. Second, teach the hitter how to get out of the way of pitches thrown at him or her. Use rolled-up socks or sponge balls and teach the hitter to turn the front shoulder in and away from the pitch. Players will be surprised at how easily they

This follow-through illustrates a hitter who is attempting to lift and pull the ball.

120

can get out of the way. *Common results:* Strikeouts, weakly hit balls to the opposite field, a lot of called strikes.

Are you hoping to get a hit? Hitters should never hope to get a hit, but rather they should know they're going to get a hit each time up. If the hitter is hoping, it's evidence of diminished confidence. *Common results:* Called strikes, bases on balls, late swings on pitches, balls primarily hit to the opposite field.

Another side of the mental aspect that may influence hitter performance is players putting unnecessary pressure on themselves. If they approach every at-bat with the mentality that getting a hit is a life-or-death situation, they may become victims of their own thought. Stress speeds up the heart rate, making it difficult to relax and allow the body to function effectively.

Young hitters have to understand that hitting is very difficult and that failure is simply part of the craft. The very best hitters in the world bat .300, meaning seven out of ten times they're making an out. Those who learn to deal with failure productively will allow that failure to make them better. And those who can't handle failure will ultimately flatline, allowing the poor at-bats to get the best of them. Eventually, less talented players will surpass them in performance.

Lack of discipline is another common mistake made by hitters. They become so anxious to swing the bat that they swing at difficult pitches in and out of the strike zone. Hitting is tough enough on its own. Swing at a bad pitch and it becomes seemingly impossible.

The percentage of sharply hit balls rises dramatically when hitters swing at good pitches. Hitters that are patient and work the count to their favor usually hit for better averages. They are "selectively aggressive." They look for pitches in certain locations early or ahead in the count, and if the pitch is there, they attack. If it's outside of their preferred location, they take the pitch.

Chasing pitches out of the strike zone makes hitting more difficult than it needs to be.

Mechanical Mistakes

Often slumps are caused by flawed mechanics. Refer back to Chapter 2 where the mechanics of hitting are explained. Go through a checklist of each step of the swing in an attempt to locate the problem. In working with thousands of hitters, I can say with great confidence that 90 percent of mechanical flaws occur before the forward swing even starts. The majority of faults rests in the stance or a preswing movement.

Below is a list of the 10 most common faults young hitters make. By identifying the problem, the hitter can begin to iron out the flaw through tee work, soft toss, and extra batting practice.

121

- *Striding open.* The front foot steps away from home plate making the hitter susceptible to middle and outside strikes. This usually stems from fear of the ball or trying to pull every pitch.
- *Striding closed.* As a remedy for striding open, coaches often advise hitters to stride closed (or toward home plate). This now makes the hitter susceptible to inside strikes and drains

the swing of power. The hips get blocked and are unable to forcefully rotate, which is the key to increased bat speed and power.

- *Striding late.* Hitters often wait to see if the pitch is a ball or strike before taking their step. The forward swing cannot start until the front foot is down. If the stride is late the swing (and barrel of the bat) will be late to the ball.

- *Drifting.* A major problem with hitters of all ages is drifting. The hitters shift their weight onto their front foot as the stride foot lands. This forces them to swing with their upper body only and reach for pitches. Inside strikes will beat these hitters consistently. Also, the head (and eyes) move forward

This is an example of a hitter who wraps his bat. From his stance position, the hitter moves his hands up and behind his head, creating a long path to the ball.

when a hitter drifts, which makes it tougher to track the ball and recognize balls and strikes.

- *Wrapping the bat.* As the hands move back to load up for power, the bat wraps behind the hitter's head. This creates a very long path for the bat to meet the ball out in front of home plate. The hands have to first unwrap before delivering the barrel to the ball. The hands should move back, but the bat angle should not cock behind the head.
- *Laying the hands off.* As the hands move back to load up, the hands lay the bat flat (parallel to the ground). From this position, the hitter slings the bat at the ball instead of firing the barrel.

Here, the batter lays his hands off just before starting his forward swing. This creates a long swing that drags to the ball, rather than one that is fired with authority.

- *Dropping the hands.* Most observers can easily pick out an uppercut, but that upward path happens for a reason. If the hands drop down during the preswing, they have no choice but to come up at the ball with the bat. If you see an uppercut swing, check the hand position before the swing. It's either that or the hitter is trying to lift everything.

- *Opening the front shoulder prematurely.* When the lead shoulder rotates open to initiate the swing, the path of the swing will pull off or away from the ball. This also takes the hitter's eyes off the ball prematurely. When hitters are "pulling their head out" or "taking their eye off the ball," it's because the front shoulder takes the head that way. Hitters never take their eye off the ball because they're bored, it's because their front shoulder pulls their eyes away from the pitch. Hitters usually open their front shoulder for one of two reasons: (1) They're trying to pull everything with power. (2) They don't feel as if they're quick enough to catch up to the pitch so they attempt to get the barrel out quicker with their upper body.

- *No pivot (or hip rotation).* The back foot fails to pivot, which does not allow the hips to rotate. Hip rotation is extremely significant to the swing. It enhances bat speed and power, and clears a path for the hands to bring the barrel directly to the ball rather than casting around the body. Hitters must be taught that their swing entails more than just using their hands and wrists. The hips, lower back, and legs generate maximum force.

- *Rolling the top hand prematurely.* A monumental error that causes a healthy amount of ground balls. Instead of staying through the ball with their hands in the palm-up, palm-down position, the hitter rolls the top hand over as contact is made. This raises the barrel slightly, resulting in the top of the baseball being struck rather than the middle. Ground ball. The hands should remain palm-up, palm-down just before, during, and after contact. The top hand rolls over after contact is made. It's the difference between hitting the ball and driving it.

This swing raced up and out of the hitting zone too quickly, causing the batter to catch the top of the ball. The result is a chopped ground ball. This is often caused by rolling the top hand prematurely, rather than staying through the ball.

Stretching Out the Hot Streak

When things are going well, it's sometimes best to give it very little attention—enjoy it, but refrain from overanalyzing your success.

125

Some streaks are born of a specific thought at the plate. For example, hitters might think about trying to hit everything to the opposite field. If that approach is working, they should stick with it. Or hitters might feel confident enough to hit deep in the count. They take pitches early and get into a rhythm during the at-bat. If seeing a lot of pitches is what's working, then stick with it.

The idea is to be loyal to what is producing successful results. When hitters commit to a plan and believe in it, their level of confidence escalates. One point to watch out for is that while confidence is welcome, overconfidence becomes threatening. Batters should never be so self-assured that they fail to respect their opponent or stray from their individual work. Even in the midst of a hot streak, hitters should remain focused in batting practice and pay attention to the pitcher's patterns during the game. Cockiness makes hitters vulnerable.

Pitchers

Working with pitchers during the season is a little tricky. Batters can take swing after swing during batting-practice sessions, but there are limitations to what pitchers are able to do. They're pitching during the week, and most play other positions in games where they are not pitching. To stay fresh and avoid frequent soreness, pitchers can't throw a massive number of pitches between starts.

That said, pitchers will have some kinks to work out during the season and also must maintain arm strength. Pitchers should undertake some form of throwing every day. It's the only way to strengthen the throwing arm and develop muscle memory in their throwing mechanics.

Below is a simple in-season throwing program designed by author and college coach Randy Voorhees. Use this as a sample rep-

At least one coach on the staff should pay special attention to the pitchers on the team.

resentation of the minimum amount of work a pitcher should assume. Bullpen sessions should be performed at something less than maximum exertion.

Monday	Pitch six innings in a game (based on the total number of pitches thrown)
Tuesday	Play catch (40 to 50 feet) for 10 to 15 minutes
Wednesday	Long toss (30, then 60, then 90 feet) for 10 to 15 minutes
Thursday	Go to the bullpen mound and practice mechanics
Friday	Play catch for 10 to 15 minutes
Saturday	Long toss for 10 to 15 minutes
Sunday	Rest

Correcting Mistakes

Every pitcher is going to have good outings and bad outings during the season. The scale tips heavily toward the good outings for the better pitchers (obviously), but the point is, don't overreact if a pitcher gets hit around in a game or struggles with command. Pedro Martinez gets knocked around from time to time. Greg Maddux began the 2003 season 0–3 with a 11.05 ERA. Roger Clemens lost 155 games before winning number 300. There are times when pitchers are off their game, and there are other times where they simply have to tip their cap to the hitters.

127

The time for concern is when a pitcher experiences a string of bad outings. When this occurs, determine if there are any obvious patterns. Are a lot of pitches up in the strike zone? Is the pitcher constantly working from behind? Are bases on balls contributing to losses? Can a fair amount of the struggles be attributed to the defense behind the pitcher? Make sure enough information is gathered before suggesting adjustments.

Like hitters, problems may be rooted upstairs. Ask the pitcher some questions to see if prepitch thoughts are contributing to the problem.

Are you trying to strike everybody out? This is a common thought and mistake on the part of young pitchers. The pitcher's job is to make hitters swing the bat, put the ball in play, and give their defense opportunities for outs. Poor field conditions and mediocre fielders are a reality in Little League baseball, but overthrowing and walking hitters presents no chance for outs at any level of play.

Are you focusing on getting strike one? Many hitters are coached to take the first pitch; to see a pitch before getting offensive. Pitchers should take advantage of this. Concentrating on and getting strike one puts the pitcher in the driver's seat. The hitter is now at the mercy of swinging at what the pitcher gives him or her. Emphasize pitching from a 0-1 count rather than 1-0.

128

Trying to throw too hard (overthrowing) causes the lead shoulder to fly open prematurely. When the lead shoulder opens early, it reduces velocity and places unnecessary strain on the pitching arm.

Are you aiming or trying to guide the ball into the strike zone? Of course pitchers have a target in mind and sight as they execute their delivery, but they have to *throw* the ball to that target. Aiming the ball disrupts the flow of pitching mechanics. Tension enters the delivery and reduces arm speed and consistency. The pitcher must remain relaxed and athletic to maintain command and pitch velocity.

Are you throwing to a specific part of the strike or just the strike zone in general? The more specific pitchers can be with their objective, the better their command becomes. Instead of throwing to the middle of home plate, have them throw to one side of the plate or the other. Pitchers might surprise you with how precise they can be if you just ask them to focus on a more specific target. Throwing to the edges of the plate makes the life of a hitter much more difficult.

Are you afraid of hitting the batter? This is a common thought among Little League pitchers, especially when they've recently hit a batter with a pitch. First, it's part of the game and a mistake that occurs with every pitcher who has ever toed the rubber. Emphasize focusing on the catcher's glove and blocking out the hitter in the batter's box. Like Hall of Fame pitcher Steve Carlton used to say, "Pitching is simply an elevated game of catch."

As far as pitching mechanics are concerned, go through a checklist of each stage of the delivery, discussed in Chapter 3. Make sure the pace of the delivery is relaxed and that the pitcher maintains balance throughout the motion. Take note of the distance or direction of the stride. It is often the primary reason why pitches are consistently up, down, inside, or outside.

The biggest mistake pitchers make is that they "rush out" with their body before delivering the pitch. Their upper and lower body jump out toward home plate, while their pitching arm drags behind. This results in pitches being up and to the throwing-arm side out of the strike zone. Rushing out doesn't allow the arm to catch up, and instead of the hand staying on top of the ball and firing downward, the hand slides underneath the ball and flattens out the pitch. If you see pitchers rushing out, ask them if they are trying to create more velocity, the number-one reason why this mistake occurs.

Fielders

The primary focus of coaches customarily revolves around hitting and pitching during the season. Infield and outfield defense receives minimal attention. This is a colossal error in judgment. Teams who can catch and throw the baseball, especially at the Little League level, win games. A young team that keeps the opposition to three outs per inning will come out on top more often than not. Squads that give away outs are subject to big numbers on the scoreboard.

Defensive play suffers during the season simply because players don't get enough repetitions between games. Practice time is limited due to the game schedule. Infielders don't receive as many ground balls and outfielders see far fewer fly balls. Fielding is a skill just like hitting or pitching, and if players don't get their reps, they'll lose a degree of consistency and confidence.

Before games, after games, and certainly in practice, hit as many ground balls and fly balls as possible to players. Even if they're

Work on different types of ground balls in practice, such as slow rollers. Players will become more comfortable when a slow ground ball is hit to them in a game, and more likely to make an aggressive play.

playing solid defense, it will keep their skills sharp and confidence level high. If they're struggling, grind it out until they right the ship.

Infielders

Every infielder should field 25 to 50 ground balls per day. Obviously, much of that responsibility lies on their shoulders. But don't expect kids to understand that. Preach the importance of individual work at home. It entails a minimal amount of time, but the benefits in competition will be obvious.

Most infielders will display some sort of weakness in their fielding. It may be balls hit to their right, left, or slow rollers. Perhaps it's something other than ground balls, such as pop-ups, force plays, or making tags. Take note during games if a particular type of play gives a player difficulty. Address the weakness with the individual and work on improving it in practice.

131

The only way to perfect backhand plays is to field them in practice.

Outfielders

As mentioned in Part 1, the efficiency of outfield play is largely based on two components: technique and judgment. Once technique is learned, it remains fairly consistent. Judgment, however, necessitates constant upkeep. A right fielder, for example, might see one fly ball throughout an entire game. If that player does not see another fly ball until the next game, he or she will lose a degree of judgment. Once that judgment has been impaired enough to misjudge a ball hit in the air, confidence is lost. And when confidence is lost, technique and efficiency follow.

Hitting fly balls to outfielders is crucial. Delegate at least 10 minutes of every practice to hitting balls to outfielders. Even better, hit balls to them before each game. This provides them with reps, but also allows them to observe the flight of the ball under the current playing conditions. Wind, sun, background, and how the ball carries at that particular field all factor into judgment. There is no substitute for seeing balls in the air right before the game.

132

Positioning

Good hands, quick feet, and a strong arm assist players in the overall makeup of being a defensive asset on the field. An aspect of defense that goes largely unnoticed is positioning. Cal Ripken Jr. had a decent arm, with decent range for a shortstop by major-league standards. Ripken, however, was one of the best shortstops in the game for a long time because he was a master at field positioning. Knowing what the pitcher was throwing, the tendencies of the hitter, and the game situation helped him position himself to glove the ball sooner than most other shortstops. Ripken's physical ability was on par with other major-league shortstops, but what set him above the rest was his attention to detail.

Attentive positioning in the field can mean the difference between a base hit and a great defensive play.

133

Little League coaches and players aren't expected to keep scouting reports on hitters and where they typically hit the ball. But the game provides plenty of information that allows fielders to take an educated guess as to where they should be positioned.

A hitter may swing through and foul off a pitch late. Move to the left if the batter is right-handed and to the right if the batter is left-handed. When a hitter pulls two consecutive fastball fouls, move a couple of steps to the pull side. Strong hitters, traditionally the 3, 4, and 5 hitters in the lineup, merit deeper play. Not only will they hit the ball farther, but they'll hit it harder, meaning it will get to infielders quicker.

Field conditions also play a role in where players position themselves. High grass or soft dirt will slow down balls hit into the infield, so players should move a step or two up and expect to charge the ball. The ball will travel faster when the grass is cut low or the dirt is hard, so they should play a bit deeper.

Outfielders should also move to the right or left if a hitter appears early or late on pitches. When the outfield grass is cut high, they really have to charge balls that get through the infield. Lastly, outfielders should constantly check the wind. Have them pick up grass and toss it in the air intermittently. They should adjust their positioning according to the direction of the wind.

The ultimate goal is to get players to move on their own. Assist them early in the season, but after a few games, stop directing them. The only way they're going to learn to do it on their own is if you leave it up to them. If they fail to reposition themselves when warranted, address it between innings or after the game.

TEAM PLAYS FOR GAME SITUATIONS

Hitting, pitching, and fielding are obvious essentials when preparing a team for the baseball season. There are other aspects of the game, however, that won't surface until actual game competition begins. Bunt coverage, first-and-third steal situations, rundowns, and cutoff relays are plays that require planning, direction, communication, and practice. Players must be coached to perform in these game situations, or they will be taken advantage of on the field. The last thing coaches want for their players is to have them unprepared for such situations and find themselves at the mercy of the opposing team.

Bunt Coverages

Defensive bunt coverage is used to defend sacrifice bunts. An offensive team institutes a sacrifice bunt to advance a runner already on base. The batter is "sacrificing" him- or herself to move a runner into scoring position. With a runner on first base, a sacrifice bunt advances the base runner to second base, which puts the runner in position to score on a base hit. With a runner on second base, a sacrifice bunt advances the runner to third base. With less than two outs, a runner on third base can score on a fly ball, ground ball, pass ball, base hit, or wild pitch.

Sacrifice bunts are usually used when the score is close in the latter stages of the game. A team that is up by a run, for example, may want to add an insurance run. A tie game, trailing by a run, or when facing a dominating pitcher are also popular times to sacrifice bunt in an effort to manufacture a run.

Runner on First Base

With a runner on first base, the bunt coverage is very simple. The first and third basemen charge toward home plate when the batter squares (or pivots) to bunt. The second baseman breaks to the left to cover first base. The shortstop shifts to the left to cover second base. The pitcher fields any ball that is bunted directly toward him or her. The catcher fields the ball on short bunts near home plate.

136

The role of the catcher is vital in bunt situations. As the only position player facing the field, the catcher must commandeer the play and call out which base to throw to. If there is a sure chance

The third baseman plays up on the grass in a bunt situation. As soon as the batter squares, he should charge forward.

of getting the lead runner at second base, the catcher should call out, "Two, Two, Two!" If there is any question about getting the lead runner, take the sure out at first base: "One, One, One!"

The third baseman must be alert to aggressive base runners. If the third baseman fields the ball and throws to first base on the bunt, he or she must immediately retreat back to third base. The lead runner might try to race from first to third if third base is not covered. If a teammate fields the bunt, the third baseman should also retreat back to third base immediately.

Runner on Second Base

There are two basic options to use with a runner on second base. In the first option, the first and third basemen charge and the shortstop breaks over to cover third base. The shortstop has to break as soon as the batter shows bunt in order to get to the base in time. The second baseman covers first base, and second base is left open.

It's very difficult to get the lead runner in this situation because there is no force at third base. The ball has to beat the runner by enough to allow the player covering to catch the ball and apply a tag. In most cases, the play is to first base to get the sure out.

The second option is to have the third baseman remain at third base. The pitcher is responsible for covering the third-base side on a bunt, the first baseman charges, the shortstop moves to second base, and the second baseman covers first. This coverage is often used when there is a quick, athletic pitcher on the mound, or a left-handed pitcher (because left-handers fall off to the third-base side in their follow-through).

Runners on First and Second Base

There are three basic options with runners on first and second base. Remember, the primary objective is to get an out. Getting a lead runner is a bonus.

The first option is to use the basic coverage. Corners (first and third basemen) charge, second baseman covers first, shortstop covers third, and second base is left open. There is a force at third on this play, so the throw does not have to beat the runner by a lot. But the fielder has to be absolutely sure he or she can make the play or you're looking at bases loaded.

The second option is to have the pitcher cover the third-base side. The third baseman stays at third, shortstop covers second, and the second baseman covers first. All bases are covered, but it's important to have an agile pitcher.

The third option is to have the pitcher cover the first-base side. The second baseman covers second base, the shortstop shifts to

When the first baseman is covering the first-base side, the second baseman runs over to cover the play at first base. He should give the first baseman a target inside the foul line (as shown).

third, and the third baseman charges. The is called the "rotation" play.

There are two things to keep in mind when coaching bunt coverage. The primary objective is to get an out. The opposition is sacrificing an out to advance runners, so your team must take advantage of that sacrifice. Second, the catcher must be vocal. The catcher can see the play develop and is the field general.

First-and-Third Steals

Runners are on first and third with one out. The batter takes the pitch and the runner on first breaks to steal second base. As the catcher releases his throw to second, the runner on third breaks for home and scores easily. This is a staple play in Little League baseball and is indefensible unless the defensive team is prepared.

Listed below are several options to defend this game situation:

- Go for the runner at second base. If your catcher has a good arm and your team is in a position to trade an out for a run, get the out.
- Fake the throw to second base and try to pick the runner off third base. The runner on third may break too early, and find him- or herself in no-man's-land on a fake throw.
- The pitcher cuts the ball off. The catcher gets up and throws as if throwing to second. (The catcher should aim for the pitcher's head.) The pitcher spears the ball and quickly throws to third (or home) to cut down the lead runner.
- Throw the ball to the shortstop breaking in toward home plate. This gives the runner (and third-base coach) the appearance that the ball is being thrown all the way to second. With the shortstop breaking in, it shortens the distance of the throw and provides a very good chance of throwing the runner out at home plate.

- Throw the ball to the second baseman breaking in toward home plate. Same rationale as stated above.
- Let the runner take second base. If you have confidence in your pitcher and defense, concentrate on getting the batter and avoid throwing the ball around.

Work on two to four of these play options in practice. It must be practiced over and over so kids will know exactly what to do during competition. Also, make sure everyone on the team (infielders, outfielders, and pitchers alike) knows the plays. You never know who will be playing where at any given time.

When the situation arises in the game, have a number or name for each play. When time is called, give the sign to the catcher and have the catcher walk in front of home plate and signal the play to the infield. Vary your plays throughout the game.

One play to run in a first-and-third steal situation is to have the shortstop run in toward the pitcher's mound to cut off the throw from the catcher. If the runner from third breaks, the shortstop throws home for the out.

Rundowns

If there is any play on the baseball field that most likens itself to a circus act, it has to be rundowns. It's entertaining to watch and fun for kids, but it usually ends in disaster for the defensive team.

The number one infraction committed on this play: too many throws. The more throws by Little League players, the greater the chance of the ball being dropped or thrown away. Limit the number of throws and increase your chances of tagging out the runner.

To limit the number of throws, the defensive player with the ball has to make the runner commit to running to a base. The way to do that is to run at the base runner—hard! Force the runner to make a decision. If the runner tries to dance around in the middle, the defensive player running hard will tag the runner out. If the base runner runs hard to a base, the defensive player can then toss the ball to the teammate at the base, who will receive the ball and tag the runner out. Forcing base runners to run hard toward one base prevents them from stopping, turning around, and running in the opposite direction.

When running at the base runner hard, the defensive player should hold the ball in the throwing hand and hold it up high. This is so the teammate at the base can see the ball. Defensive players should *not* fake their throws in an effort to fool the runner. They'll end up fooling their own teammate, and when they actually deliver the throw, the teammate will be caught off guard and possibly miss the throw.

One other quick point: the player holding the base must give the teammate a throwing lane. This means that the baseman

In a rundown, the infielder with the ball must run hard at the base runner to force him to commit.

141

should never stand in a direct line with the runner. That would force the teammate to loft a throw over the head of the runner— an extremely difficult throwing option. That is much too difficult and usually results in the ball being thrown wild high. The defensive player holding the base should move to one side or the other to give the teammate a clear target to throw to. Also, shorten the distance of the rundown by coming in off the base. There is no rule that says the fielders have to stay at their base.

Work on this in practice. If you don't, it will bite you in the game. Kids enjoy this drill, so it's not difficult to maintain their attention.

Cutoffs and Relays

With a runner on second base, a single to the outfield often creates a play at home plate. Little League outfielders may not have the arm strength to reach the plate from the outfield and need the help of a teammate. An infielder must be a cutoff if a throw needs to be relayed home or thrown to an alternate base.

On balls hit to left field, the third baseman is the cutoff. The

On balls hit to the outfield fence, a cutoff play is in order.

third baseman should be positioned from up near the edge of the infield dirt to back deeper in the infield grass. Exactly where the third baseman stands depends on the depth of the outfielder and the strength of the outfielder's arm. On balls hit to center and right field, the first baseman becomes the cutoff. The first baseman's positioning also depends on the outfielder's depth and arm strength.

The catcher must be vocal on this play. If the throw is strong and on-line, the catcher should say nothing. No command means the ball goes untouched and continues its path to home plate. If the ball is off-line or is losing steam, the catcher should yell, "Cut!" The word that follows "cut" dictates where the ball is to be thrown. "Cut four!" means the cutoff player should throw home. "Cut two!" means the throw goes to second base, and so on. If the catcher simply yells, "Cut!" the cutoff player holds the ball and checks the runners on base.

On extra-base hits, the middle infielders become cutoffs for the outfielders. They run out into the outfield grass, raise their hands, and listen for the catcher's call of where the throw should go. On balls hit to left field, the shortstop is the cutoff player. On balls hit to right field, the second baseman is the cutoff player. If the ball is hit to center field, the middle infielder with the stronger arm (usually the shortstop) becomes the cutoff player.

Practicing this will not only get your team some outs during the season, but it will also stop the opponent from taking extra bases. This will pay major dividends over the course of a season.

PART 4

KEEPING IT SAFE

9

PREPARING FOR A SAFE SEASON

There is no question that injuries are going to happen on a baseball field. Any time a group of children get together for friendly competition, mishaps occur. When bats, balls, running, errant throws, and sliding are added to the mix, unintentional accidents become unavoidable.

It is the responsibility of parents and coaches, however, to minimize the risk of injury and protect players. Taking sensible precautions will eliminate a lot of unnecessary bumps and bruises. In addition, adults must be prepared and ready to act when an injury on the field does transpire. This aspect of coaching baseball is even more important than knowing when to bunt or substitute pitchers.

This section will discuss proper equipment, emergency procedures, first aid, and how to prepare and protect your players for game situations where injuries are frequently sustained.

Equipment

Baseballs

Baseballs licensed by Little League will be printed with one of two designations: "RS" (for regular season play) or "RS-T" (for regu-

SAFETY CODE FOR LITTLE LEAGUE

- Responsibility for safety procedures should be that of an adult member of the local league.
- Arrangements should be made in advance of all games and practices for emergency medical services.
- All coaches, officials, and parents should be aware of what actions to take during an emergency.
- Managers, coaches, and umpires should have some training in first aid. A first aid kit should be available at the field as well as a phone and emergency phone numbers.
- No games or practices should be held when weather or field conditions are not good, particularly when lighting is inadequate.
- The play area should be inspected frequently for holes, damage, glass, and other foreign objects.
- Only players, managers, coaches, and umpires are permitted on the playing field during play and practice sessions.
- Dugouts and bat racks should be positioned behind screens.
- Responsibility for keeping bats and loose equipment off the field of play should be that of a regular player assigned for this purpose.
- Procedure should be established for retrieving foul balls batted out of the playing area.
- During practice sessions and games, all players should be alert and watching the batter on each pitch.
- During warm-up drills, players should be spaced so that no one is endangered by errant balls.
- Regulations prohibit on-deck batters. This means no player should handle a bat, even while in an enclosure, until it is his or her time at bat. This rule applies to Little League (Majors and Minor) and Tee Ball.
- Equipment should be inspected regularly. Make sure it fits properly.

- Pitching machines, if used, must be in good working order (including extension cords, outlets, and so on) and must be operated only by adult managers and coaches.
- Batters must wear protective NOCSAE helmets during practice, as well as during games.
- Batting/catcher's helmets should not be painted unless approved by manufacturer.
- Catchers must wear a catcher's helmet (with face mask and throat guard), chest protector, and shin guards. Male catchers must wear a long-model chest protector, protective supporter, and cup at all times.
- Except when a runner is returning to a base, headfirst slides are not permitted. This rule applies to Little League (Majors and Minor) and Tee Ball.
- During sliding practice bases should not be strapped down.
- At no time should "horseplay" be permitted on the playing field.
- Parents of players who wear glasses should be encouraged to provide safety glasses.
- Players must not wear watches, rings, pins, jewelry, or other metallic items.
- Players who are ejected, ill, or injured should remain under supervision until released to the parent or guardian.

149

lar season and tournament play). The ball used must meet Little League specifications and standards. It shall not weigh less than five (5) nor more than five and one-fourth (5¼) ounces, and measure not less than nine (9) nor more than nine and one-fourth (9¼) inches in circumference. (Tee Ball: the ball may carry the words "Little League Tee Ball.")

An official Little League baseball

The label indicates that this bat is sanctioned by Little League and permitted in league play.

Bats

The bat may be either a softball or baseball bat that meets Little League specifications and standards as noted in this rule. It shall be a smooth, rounded stick and made of wood or of material tested and proved acceptable to Little League standards. It shall not be more than thirty-three (33) inches in length, not more than 2¼ inches in diameter, and if wood, not less than $^{15}/_{16}$ inches in diameter at its smallest part. Bats may be taped or fitted with a sleeve for a distance not exceeding sixteen (16) inches from the small end. A nonwood bat must have a grip or cork, tape or composition material, and must extend a minimum of ten (10) inches from the small end. Slippery tape or similar material is prohibited. No laminated bat shall be used. Colored bats are acceptable. Painted bats made of wood are not acceptable. An illegal bat must be removed.

Uniforms

All players on a team shall wear numbered uniforms identical in color, trim, and style. The official Little League patch must be affixed on the upper left sleeve of the uniform blouse. Patches are worn three inches below the left shoulder seam or raglan sleeve; one inch below seam on set-in sleeve; over left breast on sleeveless style. Any part of the pitcher's undershirt or T-shirt exposed to view shall be of a uniform solid color, not white or gray.

Gloves

The catcher must wear a catcher's mitt (not a first baseman's mitt or fielder's glove) of any shape, size, or weight consistent with protecting the hand. The first baseman may wear a glove or mitt not more than 12 inches long from top to bottom and not more than eight inches wide across the palm, measured from the base of the thumb crotch to the outer edge of the mitt. The glove may be of any weight. Each fielder other than the first baseman and the catcher may wear a glove not more than 12 inches long nor more than 7¾ inches wide, measured from the base of the thumb crotch to the outer edge of the glove. The glove may be of any weight.

The pitcher's glove shall be uniform in color, or of varying shades of the same color, and may have contrasting stitching, lacing, and/or webbing, providing the glove, lacing, or webbing is not white or gray.

The patch on the left shoulder by Little League ballplayers is worn with great pride.

First basemen are permitted to use a first baseman's glove.

No pitcher shall attach to the glove any foreign material of a color different from the glove. The pitcher may wear a batting glove on the nonpitching hand under the pitcher's glove provided the batting glove is not white, gray, or optic yellow.

Helmets

Each league shall provide in the dugout or bench of the offensive team six (6) protective helmets, which must meet the NOCSAE specifications and standards. Use of the helmet by the batter, all base runners, and base coaches is mandatory. Use of a helmet by an adult base coach is optional. Each helmet shall have an exterior warning label.

Athletic Supporters/Catchers

All male players must wear athletic supporters. Male catchers must wear the metal, fiber, or plastic type cup, and a long-model chest protector. Female catchers must wear long- or short-model

Coaches should give players assistance if their gear needs repair, especially in the case of the catcher.

153

chest protectors. All catchers must wear chest protectors with neck collar, throat guard, shin guards, and catcher's helmet, all of which must meet Little League specifications and standards. Catcher's helmet must meet NOCSAE specifications and standards. All catchers must wear a mask, "dangling" type throat protector, and catcher's helmet during infield/outfield practice, pitcher warm-up, and games. Skull caps are not permitted.

L-Screens

An L-screen is useful for coaches and parents when throwing batting practice. It protects adults from ground balls and line drives hit directly at them by hitters. Batting practice pitchers should bend down behind the screen after the pitch is released. An L-screen is essential when throwing batting practice from a shortened distance. Short-distance batting practice is extremely productive for hitters, but it reduces the reaction time for batting practice pitchers to avoid being hit by batted balls. Only coaches and parents should be permitted to throw batting practice.

First Aid

Very few people are medical professionals, but that does not excuse coaches and parents from attaining knowledge in basic first aid. By taking a position as a coach or coach's assistant, you are also accept-

HOW TO BREAK IN A GLOVE

Breaking in a new glove correctly helps players to catch the baseball with proper technique as well as greater ease.

Your objective when breaking in a glove is to create a deep pocket (in the palm of the glove). The fingers of the glove should be worked so they corral inward toward the pocket. You can accomplish this by constantly pressing downward on the fingertips of the glove and pushing inward on the thumb and pinkie finger of the glove. Remember, the outer edges of the glove should be pushed in toward the pocket. This is especially important when breaking in an infielder's glove.

The best way to break a glove in is to play catch with it, but do so with focus. Each ball should be received in the pocket of the glove. When the ball constantly hits the pocket, the inside of the glove will cave around it and develop that deep pocket you're looking for.

Players should not catch balls in the web. The pocket will close if this is a habit, and ground balls will become more difficult to field. This is a common practice of young players. They don't want to catch the ball in the pocket out of fear of hurting their palm, so instead they catch everything in the web.

Lastly, there are products you can apply to the glove that soften the leather, thus accelerating the breaking-in process. There are many different products available, but the key ingredient is anolamine. Anolamine can be found in most shaving creams, and it works very well. Rub some into the glove from time to time, and also use it when the glove gets dried out from hot weather.

154

ing responsibility for the welfare and safety of a group of children at practices and games. Courses in first aid are available through your local Red Cross affiliates. Contact information can be found in the business section of your phone book or at www.redcross.org.

The most important thing coaches and parents should do is to be prepared for an emergency. You should know when to call, who to call, and what care to provide. Providing care involves giving first aid until the emergency medical help arrives. Even if you don't have any first aid training, you can help in an emergency.

Calling 911 or the local emergency number is the most important step you can take in an emergency. Remember it's better to call when in doubt. Emergency help can be dismissed if not needed. If you or another person is attending to the victim's needs, someone else should assume responsibility for calling for emergency assistance, directing emergency personnel to the location, and providing any information about the victim and his or her injury. The sooner necessary help arrives, the better the outcome for the injured victim. Remember, it takes at least 10 minutes for emergency assistance to arrive. Be decisive and be quick.

Preparation

Preparation is essential to providing the best possible first aid care to a player or coach. At every practice, game, or team gathering, have the following on the premises:

- Medical information about each player and coach, which includes each person's emergency numbers.
- Up-to-date medical and insurance records. Inquire about any pertinent medical conditions such as allergies, asthma, diabetes, blood disorders, or heart problems.
- Know if your community is served by an emergency 911 telephone number. If it's not, look up and record the numbers for the police department and EMS and have them readily avail-

able. Emergency numbers are commonly listed in the front of the telephone book.

- A cellular telephone that is charged and working.
- Know specific directions to where you are, including landmarks and names of roads.
- Keep a fully stocked first aid kit handy on site as well as instant ice packs.
- Learn and practice first aid skills.

At every practice and game, always have an assistant in attendance. If you don't have an assistant coach, set up a rotating system where one parent volunteers to attend each practice and game. In an emergency situation, it's essential to have two adults on the scene: one to provide immediate care to the victim, and one to call and direct emergency help.

If by chance you are the only person on site, shout for help. If no help arrives, call 911 or the local emergency number. Find the nearest telephone as quickly as possible, make the call, and immediately go back to the victim. Provide first aid to the victim as necessary. Reassure the victim while helping him or her to rest comfortably until help arrives.

Recognition

Recognizing the severity of an injury and whether it warrants an emergency call can be difficult if you're not a medical expert. One rule to follow is that if you're not sure, call the emergency number for an ambulance. It's better to be safe. Also, the hospital will know the patient is arriving and his or her condition, prompting quicker attention at the hospital (as opposed to waiting in the emergency room). Listed below are life-threatening symptoms that indicate emergency assistance is absolutely necessary. Call for emergency assistance if the victim exhibits any of the following:

- Is or becomes unconscious
- Is not breathing
- Has trouble breathing or is breathing in a strange way
- Has chest discomfort, pain, or pressure that persists for more than three to five minutes or that goes away and comes back; a rapid, weak pulse; or no pulse
- Is bleeding severely
- Has pressure or pain in the abdomen that does not go away
- Is vomiting or passing blood
- Has a seizure that lasts more than a few minutes or multiple seizures
- Has a seizure and is diabetic
- Has a severe headache, slurred speech, or bleeding from the ears or mouth
- Appears to have been poisoned, or has a severe allergic reaction
- Has injuries to the head, neck, or back
- Has possible broken bones
- Has a severe eye injury
- Has an imbedded object of any kind

Non-life-threatening injuries such as bruises, sprains, muscle injuries, cuts, scrapes, and insect bites usually do not require emergency help, but may require a doctor's visit. A knocked-out tooth should be retrieved and saved in water as it can be reinserted if done quickly. Treat any bruise or swelling immediately with "RICE": rest, immobilization, cold, and elevation.

Heat-Related Illness

Baseball is primarily played in the spring and summer, and long stints in hot weather can take their toll on players. Heat cramps, heat exhaustion, and heat stroke are caused by overexposure to heat. Drinking fluids before and during workouts or game sessions is a preventative measure, but it is difficult to monitor what each player consumes before and during a practice or game.

Heat cramps are the first indicator that the body is having trouble dealing with the heat. They are painful muscle spasms that often occur in the legs and abdomen. If a player complains of cramps, have him or her rest in a cool area and drink cool water or a sports drink. Rest, fluids, and stretching out the ailing muscle area usually allow the body to recover.

Heat exhaustion is a condition more severe than cramps. Its signals include flushed skin, headache, nausea, dizziness, and/or weakness. In this situation, move the player to a cooler area and remove or loosen clothing. An environment where there is circulating air is helpful, as is applying cold water with a cloth or sponge. Give the individual small sips of cool water, and if the person's condition

Players should drink plenty of fluids before, during, and after competition.

WHAT COACHES AND PARENTS SHOULD KNOW ABOUT GOOD SAMARITAN LAWS

Accidents and injuries happen on the baseball field. The question may arise, are there laws to protect you when you help in an emergency situation?

The answer is yes. Most states have enacted "Good Samaritan" laws. These laws give legal protection to people who gratuitously provide emergency care to ill or injured persons.

When a citizen responds to an emergency and acts as a reasonable and prudent person would under similar conditions, Good Samaritan immunity generally prevails. For example, a reasonable and prudent person would:

- Move a victim only if the victim's life was endangered
- Ask a conscious victim for permission before giving care
- Check the victim for life-threatening conditions before providing further care
- Summon emergency medical personnel to the scene by calling 911 or the local emergency number
- Continue to provide care until more highly trained personnel arrive

Good Samaritan laws were developed to encourage people to help others in emergency situations. They require that the "good Samaritan" use common sense and a reasonable level of skill, not to exceed the scope of the individual's training in emergency situations. They assume each person would do his or her best to save a life or prevent further injury.

Lay responders are rarely sued for helping in an emergency. However, Good Samaritan laws protect responders from financial responsibility provided they are not deliberately negligent or reckless and do not abandon the victim after initiating care.

fails to improve or he or she becomes unconscious, call 911 or the local emergency number.

Heat stroke is the most severe heat illness and a life-threatening emergency. When heat exhaustion is ignored, heat stroke can rapidly occur. The body systems become overwhelmed by heat and begin to stop functioning. This is a serious medical emergency that can be detected by red, hot skin that is dry or moist; changes in consciousness; rapid, weak pulse; and rapid, shallow breathing.

If a player is showing signs of heat stroke, call 911 or the local emergency number immediately. In the meantime, move the individual out of the heat and loosen any tight clothing. Apply cool, wet cloths and spray the body with water. If the player is conscious, give him or her small sips of cool water to drink—about four ounces of water every 15 minutes. Let the victim rest in a comfortable position until medical help arrives.

If the player vomits, stop giving water and place the individual on his or her side to avoid choking. Watch for signals of breathing problems such as shallow or labored breaths. Keep the individual lying down and continue to cool the body in any way possible. If you have ice or cold packs, place them on the player's wrists, ankles, groin, armpits, and neck to cool the large blood vessels.

10

AVOIDING INJURY ON THE FIELD

Injuries will occur in any sport. They also happen on the playground, in the yard, and even inside the home. In baseball, there are certain plays where injuries are more commonly sustained, but there are preparatory precautions a coach can take to keep them to a minimum. Work on these plays and practice to create a safer playing field for the players.

Sliding

Baserunning is one of the least scrutinized aspects of baseball, but it's essential to a player's or team's success. A critical element to baserunning is sliding. Players like to slide, but when performed incorrectly, it produces injuries. It's important to practice proper form so players feel comfortable sliding in the game.

One of the most common errors Little League players make is using their hands to brace their fall (or slide), causing many wrist injuries. The proper technique is to throw their hands up in the air as they land on their rear ends. This obviously protects the fingers, hand, and wrist from jamming into the ground and suffering a cut or sprain.

The lead leg should be slightly bent as the player goes into the base, allowing for some cushion as the player contacts the base. Extending the leg so it's stiff can be dangerous, especially if it collides with a stationary object like the defensive baseman's leg. The toes should be pointed up to contact the base with the sole of the foot.

When to Slide

Another big mistake made by players is that they slide too late. They wait until they're a foot or two from the base and jump into

The arms and hands are raised in the air as the player slides. This protects the hands and wrists from sprains and scrapes.

their slide. If the foot collides with the base (or, even worse, with the defensive player's leg) at the beginning of the slide, ankle sprains or knee injuries can follow. Players should begin their slide at least a few feet before the base. The condition of the playing surface often influences how early or late the player should slide. Check the field conditions before the game and alert your players.

Any time there is a close play at second base, third base, or home plate, the player should slide. (A player has to slide at home on any play at the plate when the field player has possession of the ball and is waiting to make the tag.) It's safer for the runner and the defensive player. In addition, the runner will be safe more often when sliding on close plays.

Observant base runners slide to the opposite side of the base from where the defensive player is positioned. Any time runners can make the tag a longer distance for the defensive player, they have a better chance of being safe. It also assists in avoiding collisions. Teach players to take note of where the baseman is stationed

The lead leg is slightly bent, never locked or fully extended, as it reaches the base.

slide to the opposite side. (For example, if the baseman is
ᵥiving a throw on the infield side of second base, slide to the out-
ᵣ side of the base.)

When Not to Slide

Many young players have seen major-league ballplayers slide into
first base when trying to leg out a hit. This is wrong. It is too dangerous and should not be practiced. Furthermore, it takes longer to
reach first base when runners slide. They have to break out of their
sprint and slide, which takes time. They also incur friction from the
ground when they hit. Have you ever seen an Olympic sprinter slide
across the finish line? Absolutely not, because it's not the fastest
method of getting there. If it were, you would see it all the time.

Little League players are not permitted to slide headfirst. They
will be called out automatically. As players get older, headfirst sliding is condoned but not recommended as it carries too much risk
of injury. And players should never, *ever*, slide headfirst into home
plate. No matter what age or level of play, headfirst slides into home
plate are forbidden. It's one of the most dangerous plays in baseball.

Pop-Up Priorities

Teaching pop-up priorities is a tremendous responsibility of the
coach. It will avoid collisions between players and also help record
outs throughout the season. We have all seen it happen in Little
League games (and even sometimes in the major leagues). The ball
is popped up in the air. Three players converge on the spot where
the ball is descending. All of them cluster together, become spooked
at the last second, and the ball drops safely for a hit.

At least one time per week in practice, run through the "pop-up
priorities" exercise to avoid potential collisions and secure easy
outs. Put the players on the field in their positions. Substitute play-

ers should also take their customary positions. Review the rules first before hitting or tossing balls into the air. The commentary for pop-up priorities goes like this.

The shortstop and third baseman both start back for the ball, but the shortstop has priority and calls off the third baseman.

On balls hit in the air, the catcher has priority over the pitcher. If both players call for the ball, the catcher has priority. The first baseman has priority over the catcher and pitcher. The second baseman has priority over the first baseman, catcher, and pitcher. The third baseman has priority over the catcher and pitcher. The shortstop has priority over everyone in the infield.

Priority means that if the ball is hit up in the air, the player who maintains top priority is responsible for catching the ball. If the ball is hit behind first base and the first baseman calls for the ball, but then calls from the second baseman are heard, the first baseman peels away and out of the play. It's the second baseman's ball. Having players understand who has priority in the field avoids confusion, blunders, and unnecessary injuries.

Outfielders have priority over the infielders. The left fielder has priority over the shortstop and third baseman; the right fielder has priority over the first and second baseman; and the center fielder has priority over the shortstop, second baseman, and both the left and right fielder. The center fielder is the proverbial "King of the Hill" on balls hit in the air.

The outfield positions have priority over infielders because it's easier to catch a ball coming in than going back, and also because they can see everything in front of them. If an infielder hears an outfielder call for the ball, he or she should get out immediately. Calls should be, "Mine! Mine! Mine! Mine!" It should be called out loud and often.

The pitcher has priority over no one. This doesn't mean that the pitcher shouldn't try to catch balls hit in the air. Often in Little League, the pitcher is the best athlete on the field. It does mean, however, if another player calls for the ball, the pitcher should get out.

After reviewing who has priority over whom, hit or toss pop flies in open spots. Emphasize to players to call loudly for the ball, and

that if someone who has priority over them calls, to peel away from the play.

The shortstop, second baseman, and center fielder run for a short fly ball. The center fielder makes the catch because he has priority over all fielders.

Getting Out of the Way of Pitches

One of the most common flaws young hitters make is that they step away from pitches. It is one of the most difficult mistakes to correct. Simply put, when an object is thrown at maximum velocity in a person's direction, human instinct is to get out of the way. As coaches, we teach hitters to stay in there and step directly toward the person throwing it. The best method of fixing this "very normal" problem is to throw pitch after pitch after pitch to the hitter to establish a sense of comfort.

Another step is to teach hitters the correct method of getting out of the way of a pitch. This helps avoid potential injury, but also increases a hitter's confidence by knowing how to avoid getting hit.

The correct method is to roll the front shoulder inward and turn away from the pitch. With remarkable consistency, the ball will miss the hitter. Turning in also protects the face and chest. When hitters turn in the opposite direction (out to face the pitch), the face and chest area are wide open.

168

If the pitch does happen to catch the hitter that turns in correctly, the ball will hit the rear shoulder or back. It may sting, but will likely be no more than a bruise. Practice throwing tennis balls or IncrediBalls when teaching hitters how to turn away from the pitch to prevent injuries.

Bunting

Sacrifice bunts and bunting for base hits are a part of Little League, high school, and major-league baseball. It has become somewhat of a lost art with such a high premium placed on power hitting, but bunting certainly maintains its place in the game. Advancing a runner in the late innings of a close game or dropping down a drag bunt when facing a dominant pitcher can greatly benefit a team in need of offense.

Bunting should be taught and practiced at every level not only because of its function but also to ensure that it's performed properly. Injuries, especially at the Little League level, can result from exercising improper technique. Drag or push bunting can be too advanced for the majority of Little League players, so we'll focus on teaching sacrifice bunting.

There are two methods of sacrifice bunting: the square method and the pivot method. Out of

The ball is held out away from the body when bunting. This is not only important for execution, but for safety as well.

169

concern for safety, the pivot method should be employed. When using the square method, it becomes more difficult for the batter to elude an errant pitch.

After receiving the bunt sign, the player should move closer to the plate and up in the batter's box. Moving closer to the plate provides the batter with full plate coverage (the ability to bunt inside, middle, and outside strikes). Standing farther up in the box increases the chances of bunting the ball fair. It also takes away the break of a pitch from a pitcher who has the ability to throw a breaking pitch.

The front foot opens slightly and rear foot pivots when using the pivot method. The upper body leans slightly over home plate. The top hand (right hand for right-handed hitters) slides up on the bat to a point just below the fattest part of the barrel. The bottom hand slides upward to the top of the handle. This provides the hitter with much better control of the bat.

It's important that the fingers of the top hand stay behind the barrel. The ball is properly contacted well above the position of the top hand, but it's better to be safe. The batter's fingers should not be wrapped around the barrel, thus exposing the backs of the fingers to the ball. If the ball is thrown hard inside, it's possible to have the pitch strike the fingers.

Batters should attempt to bunt the ball with the very end of the bat. This deadens the ball and produces a controlled bunt. It also eliminates the risk of being hit by the pitch on the hand.

When showing bunt, batters should completely extend their arms out toward the pitcher, and then relax by allowing a little flexion (or bend) in their arms. They want to hold the bat out in front of them so their eyes can track the pitch all the way into their bat. Hitters should not hold the bat close in toward their body. First, they'll lose sight of the ball the last few inches and risk missing the pitch. Second, if the ball catches the top of the barrel and shoots up, they could be struck in the face by the ball. If the bat is out in front of them, the ball will harmlessly carry over their head.

Finally, the bat should be held at a slightly upward angle in the bunting position—that is, the barrel end is higher than the handle end. Because the batter wants to bunt the ball down on the ground, angling the barrel upward gives the hitter the best chance. Also, holding the bat level risks dropping the barrel slightly and fouling the pitch straight back or up.

Batters should practice bunting every time they take batting practice. It's the only way to establish comfort, confidence, and reliability. When hitters fail to practice and are asked to bunt in a game situation, their nervousness will diminish their ability to execute correctly and increase the risk of injury.

And, Finally, Common Sense

Baseball is a glorious game to play and coach, but keep in mind that dangers are imminent without supervision. At practice, multiple baseballs and bats can be a recipe for destruction when in the hands of enthusiastic kids. Here are a few laws of the land that can help avoid senseless accidents.

- When a team is warming up and playing catch, make sure everyone is throwing in the same direction.
- If a ball is overthrown or dropped during team throwing practice, instruct players to call out to the coach. They should *not* chase their ball, as they may run into crossfire.
- During infield practice, only one ball is in play. Do not have multiple coaches hitting to different infield positions.
- During outfield practice, only one ball is in play. Do not have multiple coaches hitting to different outfielders.
- Players always wear a helmet during batting practice.

Players having a catch should always be doing so in the same direction. Make sure they give themselves plenty of space between players when standing in a line.

- Catchers always wear a helmet, mask, and protective gear when warming up a pitcher.
- No player is allowed to swing a baseball bat at any time unless given permission by a coach.
- Always have water and ice on the premises.

Common sense keeps the risk of injury to a minimum. But make no mistake, it's up to the adults to practice sensible thought. Never assume that kids will be wary of danger, because their focus is only on playing and having fun. And that's where it should be.

Index